Indexing

CHANDOS

INFORMATION PROFESSIONAL SERIES

Series Editor: Ruth Rikowski
(email: Rikowskigr@aol.com)

Chandos' new series of books are aimed at the busy information professional. They have been specially commissioned to provide the reader with an authoritative view of current thinking. They are designed to provide easy-to-read and (most importantly) practical coverage of topics that are of interest to librarians and other information professionals. If you would like a full listing of current and forthcoming titles, please visit our website www.chandospublishing.com or email info@chandospublishing.com or telephone +44 (0) 1223 499140.

New authors: we are always pleased to receive ideas for new titles; if you would like to write a book for Chandos, please contact Dr Glyn Jones on email gjones@ chandospublishing.com or telephone number +44 (0) 1993 848726.

Bulk orders: some organizations buy a number of copies of our books. If you are interested in doing this, we would be pleased to discuss a discount. Please contact on email info@chandospublishing.com or telephone +44 (0) 1223 499140.

Indexing

From thesauri to the Semantic Web

PIERRE DE KEYSER

Oxford Cambridge New Delhi

Chandos Publishing
Hexagon House
Avenue 4
Station lane
Witney
Oxford OX28 4BN
UK
Tel: +44 (0) 1993 484726
Email: info@chandospublishing.com
www.chandospublishing.com

Chandos Publishing is an imprint of Woodhead Publishing Limited

Woodhead Publishing Limited
80 High Street
Sawston
Cambridge CB22 3HJ
UK
Tel: +44 (0) 1223 499140 ext. 130
www.woodheadpublishing.com

First published in 2012

ISBN 978-1-84334-292-2 (print)

ISBN 978-1-78063-341-1 (online)

British Library Cataloguing-in-Publication Data.
A catalogue record for this book is available from the British Library.

Typeset by RefineCatch Ltd, Bungay, Suffolk

Contents

List of figures

List of abbreviations

AACRII	Anglo-American Cataloguing Rules, 2nd edition
AAT	Art and Architecture Thesaurus
ANSI	America National Standards Institute
BISAC	Book Industry Standards and Communication Classification
BS	British Standards
BM	Broader Mapping
BT	(in thesauri) Broader Term
BTG	(in thesauri) Generic Broader Term
BTI	(in thesauri) Broader Term of Instance
BTP	(in thesauri) Partitive Broader Term
CBIR	Content Based Image Retrieval
CDWA	Categories for the Description of Works of Art
CIP	Cataloguing in Publication
CONA	Cultural Objects Name Authority
CT	Conservation Thesaurus
DC	Dublin Core
DC-ED	Dublin Core Education Application Profile
DCMI	Dublin Core Metadata Initiative
DDC	Dewey Decimal Classification
DTD	Document Type Definition
EAD	Encoded Archive Description
EBNF	Extended Backus–Naur Form
ETD-MS	Metadata Standard for Electronic Theses and Dissertations

EQ	Equivalence
GEM	Gateway to Educational Materials
GS	(in thesauri) Generic Structure
IFLA	International Federation of Library Associations
ISBD	International Standard Bibliographic Description
ISO	International Organization of Standardization
KM	Knowledge Management
KWIC	Keywords In Context
LCC	Library of Congress Classification
LCSH	Library of Congress Subject Headings
LISTA	Library, Information Science and Technology Abstracts
LOM	Learning Object Metadata
MADS	Metadata Authority Description Schema
MARC	Machine Readable Cataloguing
MeSH	Medical Subject Headings
METS	Metadata Encoding and Transmission Standard
MODS	Metadata Object Description Schema
MPEG	Moving Picture Experts Group
NISO	National Information Standards Organization
NM	Narrower Mapping
NT	(in thesauri) Narrower Term
NTG	(in thesauri) Generic Narrower Term
NTI	(in thesauri) Narrower Term of Instance
NTP	(in thesauri) Partitive Narrower Term
OAI-PMH	Open Archives Initiative Protocol for Metadata Harvesting
OCR	Optical Character Recognition
ONIX	Online Information Exchange Standard
OWL	Web Ontology Language
PDF	Portable Document Format
QBIC	Query by Image Content
QBSE	Query by Semantic Example
QBVE	Query by Visual Example

RDA	Resource Description and Access
RDF	Resource Description Framework
RM	Related Mapping
SBD	Shot Boundary Detection
SGML	Standard General Markup Language
SKOS	Simple Knowledge Organization System
TAO	Topics, Associations and Occurrences (in topic maps)
TEI	Text Encoding Initiative
TGM	Thesaurus for Graphical Materials
TGN	Thesaurus of Geographical Names
TIE	Text Information Extraction
TT	(in thesauri) Top Term
U	(in thesauri) Use
UDC	Universal Decimal Classification
UF	(in thesauri) Used For
UF+	(in thesauri) Used For . . . and . . .
ULAN	Union List of Artist Names
USE+	(in thesauri) Use . . . and . . .
VRA Core	Visual Resources Association Core Categories
W3C	World Wide Web Consortium
X	(in thesauri and subject heading lists) See From
XML	eXtensible Mark-up Language

Preface

An introduction to the world of indexing

This book is the result of a course I have been teaching for a few years now in a library school. The rather vague curriculum plan says that it should deal with 'indexing systems', which should mean something like 'things other than subject headings and thesauri'. This allowed me to explore with an open mind what is happing in the world of indexing.

Gradually I discovered some fascinating new trends in indexing, especially in the domain of automatic indexing. I also learned that some of the newer phenomena on the Web, e.g. tagging, had everything to do with indexing and that a lot of interesting research is being done in this field. Some of the tools I have been using for more than a decade now, such as search engines of web directories, have their own indexing methods and strategies. Metadata standards, which normally only get our attention when we are dealing with the formal description of documents, all deal in some way or another with subject indexing too. They will become more and more important because the realization of the Semantic Web will rely on structured data.

Most of the research in these fields involves engineering sciences and consequently most of the research papers are full of formulas, which must discourage many an interested librarian or layman. In this book I try to convey the essence of some of the new trends in indexing without the pure technical aspects. When possible, I also refer to websites where advanced indexing tools may be seen at work. This is not always easy because most of the applications are integrated in commercial products and are not available for a broad public. Some of the examples do not have a spectacular interface, but the indexing techniques behind it may be revolutionary. The reader is then asked to make an abstraction of the interface and try and see what lies behind it.

Chapter 1 gives a brief overview of traditional (library) indexing tools: subject headings and thesauri. This overview is needed as a background for the next chapters. In Chapter 2 the arguments of supporters and opponents of automatic indexing are confronted. The chapter also focuses on the indexing traditions at the Library of Congress. The discussion about the sense of traditional indexing is not without importance because of the fact that what happens at the Library of Congress has consequences for libraries all over the world. Chapter 3 then gives some insight into the techniques that are used for automatic text indexing. This chapter is kept rather short because I did not want to confront the reader with all the mathematics that automatic text indexing requires.

In Chapter 4 we look at the fascinating world of image indexing. Because of the popularity of image sites and because of the massive presence of images on the Web, image indexing has a great future – we find some of the more advanced techniques now integrated in a common search engine like Google. Chapter 5 tries to explain how automatic indexing of moving images works. Although a lot of research is still going on in the field, some of the results can already be seen freely on the Web, which is also true of the automatic indexing of music covered in Chapter 6.

Taxonomies and ontologies are the subject of Chapter 7. Librarians may see them as old wine in new cases, but are they really? Chapter 8 gives an overview of the most popular metadata standards with respect to the library world. Special emphasis is given to how these standards deal with subject indexing and to the consequences of the fact that so many standards have emerged during the last two decades. In Chapter 9 we turn to tagging: it confronts us with a massive amount of uncontrolled indexing. The library world is embracing it as a way to engage patrons in its catalogues, but tagging is also studied for its potential to index a large part of the Web.

Chapter 10 is a short introduction to 'topic maps', one of the alternatives to traditional indexing, while the indexing of the Web is the subject of Chapter 11. It looks not only into manual forms of Web indexing but also into the mechanisms behind the most popular search engine of the moment, Google. Indexing here becomes ranking of results. The final chapter tries to understand what the realisation of the Semantic Web has to do with indexing and what the Semantic Web has to do with traditional indexing.

I have written this book with the intention of introducing the interested reader – information professional or layman – to the concepts, traditions and evolving trends in indexing. The advent of electronic storage and distribution media, culminating (for now) in the form of the World Wide Web, has turned this field into a challenging and vital area for research and development. Armed with the knowledge and ideas I am presenting in this book, I hope that the reader will be able to appreciate and utilise indexing methodologies, be motivated to learn more about them and perhaps even become professionally involved with them.

About the author

Pierre (Piet) Emmanuël de Keyser is currently head librarian of the Leuven University College (Belgium). He has a Master's degree in languages, in philosophy and in library science. At the beginning of his career he was a language teacher (Dutch and German) in several secondary schools. Since 1982 he has been a librarian, and since 2005 he combines that job with teaching several courses on indexing, classification, cataloguing and library automation in the library school of Genk (Belgium). During the past 30 years he has published many articles on the history of Dutch literature, on philosophy and on library science, most of which is in Dutch and some in English. As a member of the library expert group of VLIR-UOS, i.e. the Flemish University Development Cooperation, he is involved in library automation projects in two universities in Ethiopia.

The author may be contacted at his address:

Leuven University College
Library
Hertogstraat 178
3001 Heverlee
Belgium

E-mail: piet.de.keyser@khleuven.be
Website: *http://www.personeel.khleuven.be/~pikey*

Introduction to subject headings and thesauri

Finally, the thesaurus is like a taxonomy on steroids.

(Gene Smith [1])

Abstract: This chapter provides an introduction to traditional controlled vocabularies, i.e. subject headings and thesauri. Both are highly used in libraries, but only for thesauri are standards still updated. The main difference between both kinds is that subject headings are precoordinate and thesauri are postcoordinate. Notwithstanding this, basic rules can be formulated that apply to both types. This chapter also deals with some practical aspects of controlled vocabularies, i.e. where they can be found, how they can be created or maintained. The purpose of this chapter is not to treat controlled vocabularies in depth, but to give the reader a general overview as a reference point for the next chapters.

Key words: controlled vocabularies, thesauri, subject headings, thesaurus software, precoordinate, postcoordinate.

Introduction

Libraries use more than one system to tell their patrons what a document is about – and they mostly use a mix of different instruments. A traditional library, whose main activity consists of collecting books and keeping them at the disposal of the public, will classify them according to a classification scheme, e.g. the Dewey Decimal Classification (DDC), the Universal Decimal Classification (UDC), or the Library of Congress Classification (LCC), etc. In a classification each subject is represented by a code; complex subjects may be expressed by a combination of codes. In fact this should be enough to express the contents of a document, and a flexible classification, e.g. UDC, allows the expression of each subject adequately, no matter how specific it may be.

The reality, however, is that libraries see classification mainly as an instrument to arrange their books on the shelves, as the basis for the call number system, and as a consequence of this a rich and very detailed classification like UDC is reduced to a scheme with broad classes because of the simple fact that the long string of numbers and characters of a detailed UDC code does not fit onto a relatively small book label; moreover, every librarian knows that only a few readers have any idea what is hidden behind the notations of the library classification. Frankly, the readers do not care; they just want to know where to find the book they need.

In order to convey what a document is about, most libraries also describe its content in words, which they find in a list of 'subject headings' or in a 'thesaurus'. Both are called 'controlled vocabularies', as opposed to 'non-controlled' vocabularies, i.e. keywords assigned to documents which are not based on any predefined list and are not based on any standards.

Online databases also use more than one instrument to tell their public something about the subject of the documents they contain. Let us look at an example from the LISTA (Library, Information Science and Technology Abstracts) database, a database about library science (*http://www. libraryresearch.com*). An entry for an article by David Erdos entitled 'Systematically handicapped: social research in the data protection from work', published in the journal *Information & Communications Technology Law* in 2011, is enriched with four controlled subject terms:

Data protection–Law and legislation

Electronic data processing

Data integrity

Computer security software

It also gets one 'geographic term' ('Great Britain') and no fewer than 14 'author-supplied keywords': 'academic freedom', 'covert research', 'data export', 'data minimization', 'data protection', 'ethical review', 'freedom of expression', 'historical research', 'informational self-determination', 'personal data', 'privacy', 'regulation', 'research governance', 'subject access'. Moreover, the database contains an abstract of more than ten lines of text. A lot could be said about the relations between these four kinds of indexing for one and the same article, and they have indeed been the subject of a few studies. From an economical point of view we could easily jump to the conclusion that articles with abstracts can do with fewer added index terms because the abstracts would contain many significant words or word combinations which would make excellent search keys. Mohammad Tavakolizadeh-Ravari, an Iranian scholar who presented his dissertation at the Humboldt University in Berlin, showed that the opposite is true. For Medline, the world's leading medical database, he calculated that articles with abstracts received more subject headings than those without abstracts [2]. The indexers probably regard those articles as more important and the abstracts help them in finding suitable index terms. The possible economical arguments seem to be of no importance.

In this era of social networking, libraries offer their public the possibility to add their personal 'tags' to the description of documents in the catalogue. This opens the door for uncontrolled indexing, and although libraries embrace the interaction with the public and although they complain about the costs of controlled subject indexing, they still feel the need to provide controlled subject terms in their catalogues. Social tagging is – at this moment – just one more additional indexing method. In this book we will deal with uncontrolled indexing in more than one way, but first let us look at controlled indexing. It is not possible to go into every single detail about subject headings and thesauri; this would require at least an entire manual. However, it is necessary to provide some overview in order to create a reference point for the next chapters.

Standards for controlled vocabularies

International standards on controlled vocabularies deal mainly with thesauri. Subject headings may be developed without an explicit theory. Even huge systems can grow for decades and gain international prestige although they may be based on ad hoc decisions about each term or each category of terms. In her book on the Library of Congress Subject Headings (LCSH), Lois Mai Chan notes that in the United States, 'for many years, the closest thing to a set of rules for subject headings since Cutter was Haskin's *Subject Headings: A Practical Guide* (1951)' [3]. Although LCSH has been the most important system of subject headings since the beginning of the twentieth century, it was not until 1984 that a full manual was published. Until then every library who used LCSH was to a certain extent flying blind with it. As Alva T. Stone wrote in an article on the history of LCSH [4], 'For the first time, "outside" cataloguers were able to read the same memoranda, or instruction sheets, available to

LC cataloguers, and thus acquire the opportunity to become more consistent and improve the quality of the LCSH strings that they assigned to original-cataloguing records for the bibliographic utilities.'

In fact most of the theory, and practice, of subject headings is still based on Cutter's *Rules for a Dictionary Catalogue* from 1876 [5]. The discussions about the peculiarities in LCSH concern those points where they don't follow Cutter's rules. Masse Bloomfield formulates his criticism about this lack of theoretical foundations for indexing systems right upfront [6]: 'When indexing is the guts of the library business, where are our theoreticians? Or do the cataloguers at the Library of Congress and in our libraries across the world think that research on indexing is best done by someone else?'

This lack of theoretical foundation, and as a consequence of this the lack of consistency, makes it difficult to explain the LCSH to novice users. In her recent book, *Essential Library of Congress Subject Headings* [7], Vanda Broughton cannot hide the fact that even an experienced user does not grasp all of LCSH's secrets. Some of her ironic remarks may illustrate the frustration one has trying to explain LCSH:

> There is no explanation of this oddity, and no other comparable example; it is just another of LCSH's quirks. (Ibid. p. 57)

> However, if the distinction escapes you, you can take comfort from the fact that research has shown that most end-users and some librarians fail to appreciate these nuances of meaning. (Ibid. p. 127)

> Representation of gender is perhaps the best known example of inconsistency, largely because the lack of parity between male and female has been so frequently

criticized for its apparent political incorrectness. (Ibid. p. 140)

The important thing here is to keep calm, and think carefully about the subject and how to represent it. (Ibid. p. 161)

As usual, there are always oddities and inconsistencies in the headings, so do not worry if there are occasional things that you haven't understood properly. (Ibid. p. 227)

As is the case with many other authors, she seems to have found a benevolent attitude to LCSH as the most important controlled vocabulary in the library world: 'Nevertheless, it is an immensely useful working tool, as well as a real treasure house of the weird and wonderful in document description. It is hardly possible to open any page of LCSH without finding something to surprise and delight' (ibid. p. 12).

Thesauri do not only get more attention from standards and theory builders but they enjoy a lot more respect – although not always justifiable. The ANSI/NISO Z39.19-2005 standard states that 'a controlled vocabulary can be as simple as a short list of terms or as complex as a thesaurus containing tens of thousands of terms with a complex hierarchical structure and many different types of relationships among the terms' [8]. After reading this one might jump to the conclusion that a thesaurus is always a large system with a complex structure and that subject headings are found in rather small and simple lists. The opposite is true: subject headings are long lists, sometimes (but not always) with complex relations among terms, and most thesauri are rather small, i.e. a few thousand terms. The reason for this will be explained further in this chapter.

From about 1960 onwards, standards for thesaurus construction have been developed; they reached their climax in the 1980s where they attained the status of ISO guidelines, one for monolingual and one for multilingual thesauri:

- ISO 2788-1986: 'Guidelines for the establishment and development of monolingual thesauri'.
- ISO 5964-1985: 'Guidelines for the establishment and development of multilingual thesauri'.

Both now are actually under revision; at the time of writing only the first part of the new version has been published, ISO 25964-1: 'Thesauri and interoperability with other vocabularies. Part 1: Thesauri for information retrieval' (available at *http://www.niso.org/apps/group_public/ document.php?document_id=3119*).

At the time of writing, the second part of ISO 25964 is only available as a draft presented to the public for comments – ISO 25964-2: 'Thesauri and interoperability with other vocabularies. Part 2: Interoperability with other vocabularies'.

From the mid-1980s onward, several other standards have been published, although they merely repeated the ISO standards, e.g. BS 5723-1987: 'Guide to establishment and development of monolingual thesauri' and ANSI/NISO Z39.19-1993: 'Guidelines for the construction, format, and management of monolingual thesauri'.

All of these standards and guidelines date from a time when information was almost exclusively published in paper books and journals which were stored in physical libraries that used paper – or at least offline – catalogues. Thesauri or subject headings were also published in paper volumes. The LCSH can still be bought in six volumes, containing almost 10 000 pages. Nowadays, most printed thesauri are published on the Internet as PDF (Portable Document Format) documents, but occasionally some are still sold as books, e.g. the *Thesaurus of Psychological Index Terms* [9].

Since the end of the 1990s the need has arisen to revise these standards in the light of new phenomena that were developed, e.g. ontologies, taxonomies, topic maps:

- ANSI/NISO Z39.19-2005: 'Guidelines for the construction, format, and management of monolingual controlled vocabulary' [8].
- The International Federation of Library Associations' (IFLA) 'Guidelines for multilingual thesauri' [10].
- BS 8723: 'Structured vocabularies for information retrieval' [11].

Of course, these are only a few of the best-known standards and guidelines. Many countries have their own official or de facto standards. They not only translate the international standards into the country's language but apply them to local traditions as well. Notwithstanding that, some general principles can be formulated.

Precoordination and postcoordination

In general, subject heading systems are precoordinate and thesauri are postcoordinate. The notions of precoordination and postcoordination refer to who is making the combination between the indexing terms, the indexer or the user; in precoordinate systems the indexer combines all parts of a complex term together. Consider the following example (from the LCSH):

Education–Afghanistan–Twentieth century–Congresses

Education–Afghanistan–Congresses

Education–Afghanistan–Finance

Education–Afghanistan–History

Education–Afghanistan–History–Twentieth century

Education–Afghanistan–Maps

The indexer devises these combinations and adds them to the description of a document, e.g. in a library catalogue. He/she has to make the same combinations for all other countries, which will end up in a list of many hundreds of terms. The LCSH now contains approximately 337 000 terms, which makes it without any doubt the most extensive system in the world.

In postcoordinate systems the indexer assigns one or more terms to the description of a document, without combining them into one string of words, e.g.

Education

Finance

Afghanistan

The searcher has to make the combination while searching, e.g. the combinations

Education AND Afghanistan AND Finance

Education AND Finance

Education AND Afghanistan

will all retrieve this description, as in fact a search for each of the three terms separately will. In order to exclude this description from a search the searcher must search for e.g.

Education NOT Afghanistan

Education NOT Finance

(Finance AND Afghanistan) NOT Education

etc.

The most important subject indexing system in libraries, i.e. the LCSH, is precoordinate. Precoordination can be rather complex, as is indeed the case with LCSH: 'Terms in LCSH are precoordinated in one of four ways: subdivision, inversion, qualification, and phrase building. Each of the first three methods is indicated in the heading by a distinctive typographic means (dash for subdivision, comma for inversion, parenthesis for qualification) and initial capitalization and no following capitalization. Each method is meant to indicate a certain semantic relationship between the coordinated terms' [12].

For some years now the principles of precoordination have been under discussion at the Library of Congress – not in the first place because of the nature of it, but maybe because of the costs it involves, as is explicitly admitted in an official LC report from 2007 on the matter [13]: 'Rather than review the issue of pre- versus post-coordination, the issue perhaps should be how subject access can best be achieved for users at a cost that reduces the current expense.' The report sums up the pros and cons that were advanced over many years of discussion: precoordination is flexible and excellent for browsing through lists of subjects, but it is expensive, difficult to learn and the user does not understand the logic behind it. The report recommends that the Library of Congress should continue LCSH as a precoordinate system, but with some minor changes and a few new instruments that would help cataloguers and end-users.

General do's and don'ts in selecting index terms

The following are some general principles for any kind of indexing system. Many systems may deviate from them, not because they consider them to be wrong, but because they have reasons to give in to the opposite. We will show that the LCSH do not follow all of them, or follow them in theory, but sometimes feel the need to do otherwise. We don't do this because we want to discredit LCSH, but simply because it is, as said, the most used system in the world.

An indexing term must be as specific as possible

It is considered bad policy to have index terms that are too broad because the searcher will have to browse through too many items in order to find what he/she is looking for. If you are interested in bees and every document on any kind of insect is indexed under 'insects', you will have to go through descriptions of documents on flies, all kinds of beetles, etc. before you find one on bees. A non-specific term may be allowed for subjects that are in the periphery of the collection. A library may have a few books on computers although automation is far from its main point of interest. In that case it could be allowed to index them under some general term like 'computers' or 'automation'.

On the other hand, indexing is considered to be too specific if only one or a few documents may be found under a certain term. In 1883 the Portuguese writer Ramalho Ortigão published a book about his journey through Holland, *A Hollanda*. Indexing this book under

Holland–1883

is probably too specific (in this case it would be better to use: Holland–Nineteenth century). Indexing books on Paris in 1968 may, on the other hand, be justifiable because of the many documents on the French student revolts in that year.

Don't use multiple indexing

Multiple indexing means that the indexer attributes at the same time a specific and a general term to a document, e.g.

Geometry	and	Mathematics
Dogs	and	Animals
Flowers	and	Plants
Malaria	and	Tropical diseases

Indexers who do this argue that they want the document to be found also under the more general term, but search strategy shouldn't be their concern; it is a problem for the user or for the developer of the search software. A good system will simply allow the searcher to choose a broader term when necessary; if he/she doesn't find enough documents under 'arm chairs' the searcher can broaden the search to 'chairs' or 'furniture' if he/she wishes to do so. Especially in postcoordinate systems, it is tempting to add more terms than necessary, e.g.

Cats

Mammals

Animals

LCSH became more tolerant concerning multiple indexing, although the official policy still is to index as specifically as possible. This, too, is a case where the day-to-day use took over from theory in LCSH. As Lois Mai Chan writes [14]: 'Over the years, the Library of Congress has relaxed its general policies of not assigning a generic heading in addition to the specific heading coextensive with the content of the work. Now many works are assigned headings broader or more general than the main topic.'

Don't use indirect indexing

Indirect indexing occurs when indexers take a broader term as the first part of a subdivided index term, e.g.

Mathematics–Algebra

Buildings–Churches

Art–Painting

Europe–Germany

Again, the argument may be that the indexer wants the searcher to find the specific term under the more general one. The indexer supposes that the searcher uses a kind of hierarchical search strategy.

Inverted index terms may be seen as a variant to indirect indexing; here, too, the indexer places the more general part of the term in front:

Art, abstract

Art, American

Art, Babylonian

Normally inverted terms are considered to be too artificial, with the exception of proper names, e.g.

Joyce, James

Whitman, Walt

but in major indexes like LCSH it is still common practice, although the Library of Congress adopted a policy not to create any new inverted terms.

LCSH contain many examples of indirect and inverted terms. To justify this practice Lois Mai Chan argues that in the case of geographical terms, 'the benefit of collocating materials relating to the larger area has been considered important enough by the Library of Congress to suspend the principle of specific and direct entry' [15]. In LCSH it is common practice to construct geographical terms like

France–Paris

Florida–Okeechobee, Lake

Italy–Rome

It might be better to rely on good software that can 'explode' from a narrower term to a broader or vice versa when needed.

Be brief

Most systems set limits to the length of index terms. Of course, this is mostly a concern for the developer of precoordinate systems. Normally terms will be limited to a maximum length of four subdivisions. Postcoordinate systems are supposed to have short terms, although thesauri with long – or even extremely long – and complex terms are not exceptional, e.g.[1]

Abortion without prior consent for women with disabilities

Agricultural technologies not available for use in food production

Municipal services not provided to informal settlements

A term normally should not take the form of a description of the content of the document in a single sentence – which it does in the examples.

In subject heading systems, which by nature have longer terms than thesauri, a construction like

Education–Africa–History

is very common, but what to think about the following combinations from LSCH?

Education–Africa, East–History–Twentieth century–Chronology

Education–Africa, French-speaking West–History–Sources–Bibliography–Catalogs

Education–Aims and objectives–Dominican Republic–History–Twenty-first century

Are these too long or maybe just admissible? Of course, in the first examples the inversions in the subdivision make them more artificial. LSCH also contain terms that simply are a mouthful:

Mid-year Academic Seminar on Education and Training Programmes for and by General Medical Practitioners

Subject headings

Subject headings go back to the days of the card catalogue. The subject of a book was described in one or a few words which were typed on top of a catalogue card. This practice had some consequences. It was important to choose a subject heading that expressed the contents of the document as exactly as possible. If you would choose only a few vague or general terms you would have to retype the catalogue card as many times as you had terms, which was of course a lot of work in the days before library automation. For the same reason a system was developed to formulate complex subjects in compact form. In the LCSH one can find combinations like:

Europe–Civilization–Nineteenth century

Automobile Association (Great Britain)

Agriculture and state–Denmark–History–Nineteenth century –Statistics

The downsides of such precoordinatve indexing systems are that they tend to keep on growing rapidly and that it is labour intensive to add even obvious variations of existing terms to the list. Suppose the system has these subject headings on libraries in Jordan:

Libraries–Jordan

Libraries–Jordan–Catalogs

Libraries–Jordan–Congresses

Libraries–Jordan–Directories

Libraries–Jordan–Periodicals

The day the library gets a book on the history of libraries in Jordan a new term will be added to the list:

Libraries–Jordan–History

In this case an indexer has to suggest this as a new term; the term has to be approved and formally added to the list of allowed terms. In the early days the already long list of terms had to be retyped over and over again. In LCSH not all combinations are listed anymore; LCSH now have what is called 'free-floating subdivisions': words or combinations of words that can be combined with a vast range of other terms, e.g.

Atlases

History, military–Twentieth century

Climate

The syntax rules of the subject headings also determined which part of a multi-word term should come first, because this was important for the alphabetical classification of catalogue cards in the subject catalogue. The reader who was looking for documents on a certain subject in a card catalogue had to browse the paper cards in one of the little drawers of the catalogue. The reader would find all catalogue cards dealing with

Agriculture–Africa–History

Agriculture–America–History

under 'Agriculture' and not some under 'Africa' and others such as 'History', etc. In automated systems it would not matter which of these terms came first:

Computers–Law and legislation–France

A combined search, e.g.

France AND Computers AND Law

would retrieve all the records with these terms, no matter how they are arranged. But in a manual system you have to be rigid about the order of terms.

National and de facto standards give different rules for the construction of subject headings. A combination like

Agriculture and state–Denmark–History–Nineteenth century–Statistics

may be possible in the LCSH, but would be considered wrong in many other systems, because their rules would not allow terms to be built out of five parts and they would also forbid using a broad and a specific temporal attribute ('History' and 'Nineteenth century') at the same time.

A subject headings system may take one of the following forms:

- A simple, although probably long list of allowed terms.
- A list of allowed and disapproved terms, with a mechanism to guide the user from disapproved to the preferred terms. Mostly also references to related terms are included.

- A list in which relations between terms are documented in the way of a thesaurus.

In many cases a subject heading system uses simple relations between terms:

- Reference from a disapproved term to an approved one:

Beasts

 see   Animals

- References from a term to related terms:

Animals

 see also Human–animal relationships

 see also Sea animals

 see also Working animals

Although the 'see also' relations are not subject of strict rules, one of Cutter's laws is still valid, i.e. that a 'see also' relation may not refer to a broader term such that:

Dogs

 see also Animals

is not allowed. This may be one of the reasons why some people prefer thesauri.

Thesauri

The origins of thesauri go back to the early days of automation: computer memory was expensive and very limited, but computers made it possible to combine search terms in a way previously not possible. Instead of storing subject headings lists with combinations like

France–Geology

France–History

Germany–Geology

Germany–History

Industry–France

Industry–France–History

Industry–Germany

Industry–Germany–History

Industry–Italy

Industry–Italy–History

Italy–Geography

Italy–History

Etc.

it was much more efficient to make a list in which all terms were unique:

France

Geology

Germany

History

Industry

Italy

The same result, i.e. indexing and finding documents on the history of industry in France, etc. could be reached if the indexer added all relevant terms to the document description and if the searcher had software that allowed him to make a combination like:

Industry AND France AND History

or any possible variant of that:

France AND History AND Industry

History AND France AND Industry

France AND Industry AND History

etc.

But there is more: it is not enough to avoid precoordination and to rely on the user's ability to formulate Boolean searches, the terms we use should also be as simple as possible. It is more economical to use 'engines' and combine it with other words like 'cars' or 'aircraft' than combinations like 'aircraft engines' or 'car engines' or 'train engines'. Thesauri standards give strict rules on when and when not to split compound terms into their parts:

1. 'Aircraft engines' can be split into 'aircraft' and 'engines' because the focus of the term ('engines') refers to a part and the modifier ('aircraft') represents the whole.

2. 'Office management' should be split into 'office' and 'management' because it is the expression of a transitive action: the office is managed.

3. 'Bird migration' should be split into 'birds' and 'migration' because it expresses an intransitive action executed by the performer of the action (the birds).

The standards also contain rules when not to split:

1. Splitting is not permitted when it leads to loss of meaning or ambiguity, e.g. 'pocket knives' or 'plant food'.

2. It is not allowed when it leads to vague terms, e.g. 'first aid'.

3. It is not allowed when the modifier has lost its original meaning: e.g. when we use 'deck chairs' we don't think of chairs to put on the deck of ship.

4. It is not allowed to split when the modifier is a metaphor, e.g. 'tree structures' as opposed to 'tree leaves'.

5. It is not allowed when it contains an adjective that does not define a subclass of the focus, e.g. 'rubber ducks' are not a kind of ducks.

6. It is of course not allowed to split proper names, e.g. 'United Nations'.

7. It is not allowed when the compound term is familiar as a whole established in a certain science or trade, e.g. 'data processing'.

Of course rule number 7 opens the door for many compound terms, because each time someone can argue that a compound term is too familiar to be split or that it belongs to the jargon of a certain knowledge field.

Besides this general principle of postcoordination some other principles are important in thesauri building:

■ For every term, relations to other terms must be specified.

■ If possible, scope notes in which the use of the term is explained must be given.

Possible relations between terms are:

BT	Broader Term
BTG	Broader Term (generic)
BTI	Broader Term (instance)
BTP	Broader Term (partitive)
GS	Generic Structure
NT	Narrower Term
NTG	Narrower Term (generic)
NTI	Narrower Term (instance)
NTP	Narrower Term (partitive)
RT	Related Term

SEE   Equivalent to U (use)

TT   Top Term

U   Use

UF   Used For

UF+   Used For . . . And . . .

USE+   Use . . . and . . .

X   See From (equivalent to UF); reciprocal of SEE

It is obvious that these concepts allow us to define far more complex relations between terms than the simple 'see' or 'see also' relations of traditional subject headings systems. It is also obvious that thesauri are better suited to a specific, limited subject field than to a broad one – although universal thesauri exist. As can be concluded from the above list, i.e. from the use of top terms, a thesaurus can also include some hierarchy between terms and be based on a classification. And, in fact, the best way to construct a thesaurus is to start from a classification. In doing so, every term will have at least one broader term, i.e. one of the main classes of the classification. This is important since it is not allowed to have 'orphan terms' in thesauri (unlike in subject headings), i.e. terms without hierarchical relations.[2]

Let's consider this over-simplified classification:

1. History

    1.1. World history

    1.2. National history

2. Philosophy

    2.1. Ontology

    2.2. Logic

It is not possible to have orphan terms here: logic has philosophy as BT (which can be called the top term here) and philosophy has logic as NT and all the terms subordinated to logic have logic as BT, etc.

In addition to the relations between terms it is customary to add an explanation of how to use each one, especially in scientific thesauri, where the meaning of each term is not self-evident. This can be done in 'scope notes'. Some thesauri also use 'history notes', i.e. notes that document the history of the term: they document when it was added to the thesaurus, when it was changed, etc.; some also provide definitions, maybe instead of scope notes, maybe in combination with scope notes.

Some major subject headings systems, e.g. LCSH or Medical Subject Headings (MeSH), adopted the terminology of thesauri, which allows defining the nature of the relation between terms: one term can have a 'narrower' or 'broader' content than another. This does not mean that these subject headings systems now are thesauri. Under 'Animals' LCSH lists (among many other references):

Narrower Term: Euthanasia of animals

Narrower Term: Fortune-telling by animals

Narrower Term: Intersexuality in animals

Narrower Term: Land capability for animals

Narrower Term: Tundra animals

Narrower Term: Women and animals

All of these terms would not be acceptable in most thesauri because they are simply too precoordinate. Obviously a construction like 'Women and animals' is against the nature of a postcoordinate system. In fact, not everybody applauded when Library of Congress changed the reference system in the LCSH to a more thesaurus-like system in the 1980s. In a famous article, Mary Dykstra wrote:

Most of us have come to understand the truth of the saying that the more things change, the more they stay the same. Unfortunately, those of us who work with Library of Congress Subject Headings (LCSH) have to live with the fact that the more things change, the worse they get. LCSH have gotten worse again recently, and now things are very bad indeed [16].

Further on, she writes: 'The case cannot be made too strongly that the sorting out of xx-codes headings into BTs and RTs and the sa-coded headings into NTs and RTs will in no way turn the LCSH list into a thesaurus' and that is all too true. It is very difficult to rethink and rewrite a subject heading list into a thesaurus. Rules exist to tell what can and what cannot be considered as narrower, broader or related term and the LCSH list in many cases does not follow these rules. One of them is the 'is-a' rule: for a (generic) narrower term it should be possible to say that it is a kind of what is expressed by the broader term. A watchdog is a kind of dog, so 'watchdogs' can be used as narrower term with 'dogs'. In LCSH it is very easy to detect relations that violate this rule. For 'trees' you can find many kinds of trees as narrower terms, but also things like 'bark peeling', 'hedges', 'landscape gardening', 'photography of trees', 'tree felling', etc. Many of these terms could be related terms – but not all of them because the construction of related terms is subject to strict rules too.

Building a thesaurus can be a very painstaking task, especially when it is a multilingual one. It is usually the work of a team of subject experts and information scientists. Instead of trying to reinvent the wheel it might be a good idea to look for an existing system to use.

Creating and maintaining a controlled vocabulary

Two methods can be followed to create a controlled vocabulary: the deductive or the inductive method. The deductive method starts from an inventory of a certain domain of knowledge and tries to sum up all relevant index terms concerning it. This can be done before the actual indexing of documents begins. The inductive method creates index terms during the process of indexing; new terms are only introduced when they are needed to index a document. Usually a combination of the two methods will be applied.

In his dissertation, Mohammad Tavakolizadeh-Ravari calculated that for the inductive method initially 1600 documents would be needed to create the essence of a usable system like the MeSH and that a new term will be necessary each time 250 new documents were added to the database [2].

Any new term added to the system must be discussed by a group of subject and technical experts, which not only means that creating and maintaining a controlled vocabulary is a laborious and expensive matter, but also that it is an illusion that one person could do this. It surprises me that students in library science programmes are allowed to take the creating of a controlled vocabulary as the subject of their theses or that eager librarians try to construct a system from scratch in their spare time; this is bound to fail.

A more feasible way to create a system is starting from an already existing one and joining forces with another team. In order to do so, it is necessary to know where to look for one.

How to find subject headings and thesauri

At this moment the Taxonomy Warehouse is the most complete collection of subject headings systems and thesauri (*http://www.taxonomywarehouse.com*). The site does not make a distinction between thesauri, subject headings, classifications, taxonomies, ontologies, etc. All are called 'taxonomies' and are treated equally as they are considered to be inspiration sources to build one's own knowledge system. In the middle of 2011 the website got a new look and the terminology changed from 'vocabularies' to 'taxonomies', which is more in the line of the whole site. This illustrates that knowledge workers are more interested in what they can do with all those systems than in the subtleties of the distinctions between them. Many of the thesauri or subject headings lists you can find on this website are commercial ones and cannot be downloaded for free. The forms in which these systems come are also very different: they may be a database, a PDF file, a website or an XML file, etc.

Other lists of thesauri can be found on the Internet, mostly as collections of examples for library training programmes.

Thesaurus software

Years ago thesauri and subject heading systems were constructed manually. We could refer to those days as the 'shoe box era'. According to an anecdote in an article by Jean Aitchison and Stella Dextre Clarke [17] on the history of thesauri, in the 1960s the whole content of the Thesaurofacet thesaurus was kept and maintained in shoe boxes: 'In the case of Thesaurofacet, the alphabetical section was held in a series of 20 or more shoe boxes, containing cards for 16 000 descriptors and 7000 non-descriptors. Any changes to relationships between the terms involved hand-alteration of the first term, and then a walk across the room to make reciprocal changes to the relevant term record in another box.'

Software especially for thesauri was developed that takes care of reciprocal relations between the descriptors, for each broader term must have its narrower term and vice versa. Without such software the developers indeed have to walk around a room full of shoe boxes in order to maintain all corresponding relations. Mainly two kinds of thesaurus software packages can be found: those which are part of another software package, e.g. document database software, and those which can operate as stand-alone programmes. Obviously most thesauri will be part of a database and consequently the software by which they are created and maintained will also be part of a database application. Notwithstanding this, standalone thesaurus software can still be of use in some situations:

- A thesaurus can be created before the definitive choice of a database software has been made. In this case the thesaurus developers don't have to wait until the database package is chosen and installed; they can go ahead with their work. This can be a good solution provided that the result can be converted to a general standard like XML and that the future database software will be able to read this. Unfortunately not many of these standalone thesaurus packages are in the field of freeware; most are rather expensive.

- Some integrated library systems and database packages have the possibility to integrate a thesaurus as a search facility, but do not offer any instruments to create and maintain the thesaurus itself. All over the world, and especially in developing countries, many libraries and documentation centres use some kind of software of the ISIS family, for many reasons: it is freeware, it is supported by UNESCO (United Nations Educational, Scientific and Cultural Organization), there is huge expertise on this kind of software in e.g. Latin America, etc. Some of these software packages can integrate a thesaurus, but normally that thesaurus has to be created by a dedicated programme like MTM-4, which is also one of the ISIS applications.[3]

To get an idea of how a thesaurus software works, one can usually download and install a demonstration version of a package. It will allow the user to create a certain number of terms or it will offer full use during a limited period of time. A very simple package, Thew33 (see Figure 1.1), which can satisfy a first curiosity, can be found at the website of Tim Craven, a former professor in information sciences at the

Figure 1.1 Screenshot of Thew33 thesaurus software (*http://publish.uwo.ca/~craven/freeware.htm*)

University of Western Ontario, Canada (*http://publish.uwo. ca/~craven/freeware.htm*).

One of the most complete lists – although slightly outdated – can be consulted on the website of Leonard D. Will and Sheena E. Will, two independent consultants with roots in the library world (*http://www.willpowerinfo.co.uk*).

Multilingual thesauri

Some subject heading systems were translated into other languages, e.g. LCSH has a Spanish version, but the vast numbers of terms and the complicated subdivisions make it difficult to translate them. On the other hand thesauri, with their limited amount of terms and their tradition of breaking up compound terms into stems, are far more suitable for translation.

The ISO 5964 standard from 1985 already dealt with multilingual thesauri, and in 2005 the IFLA also published its 'Guidelines for multilingual thesauri' [10]. The main difficulty in creating a multilingual thesaurus is finding a solution for those cases where a term in one language does not correspond exactly with a term in another language. The French 'enseignement' can mean 'teaching', 'education', or 'instruction'. The German 'Geschwister' can be translated into 'siblings' in English but does not have a corresponding term in Dutch, where the only way to translate it is to say 'brothers and sisters'. For German a thesaurus term can be created like:

Geschwister

NT Brüder

NT Schwestern

If we want full correspondence between the two languages in the thesaurus we would have to resort to artificial solutions, which in this case would involve allowing more precoordination, a solution that is against the nature of thesauri:

Broers en zusters

NT Broers

NT Zusters

Another way to handle this is to settle for a non-symmetrical point of view and to allow blanks to appear in the other language when necessary.

It is obvious that creating a multilingual thesaurus is an enormous work and involves a whole staff of language experts. Nevertheless, impressive multilingual thesauri have been created, in some cases in more than ten languages. Some examples are:

- The UNESCO Thesaurus [18]: in English, French, Spanish and Russian.
- The UNBIS Thesaurus [19] from the United Nations in six languages.
- The AGROVOC Thesaurus [20] from FAO in 19 languages.
- The EuroVoc Thesaurus [21] of the European Union in 24 languages.

Interoperability between vocabularies

ISO 25964-2 goes one step further; it addresses interoperability between thesauri and other systems, i.e. classifications, taxonomies, subject heading schemes, ontologies, terminologies, authority lists, synonym rings, etc. Although it is still a draft at the time of writing (Spring 2012), it is clear that it is revolutionizing the way we look at thesauri. It introduces a whole set of new relations:

EQ (Equivalence)

BM (Broader Mapping)

NM (Narrower Mapping)

RM (Related Mapping)

Mappings between some LC classificaion notation and a LCSH term could be coded as follows:

DK40 EQ Soviet Union–History

or   DK 40 NM Feudalism–Russia

Relations will of course be very complicated, since there are fundamental differences between systems. If we want to map a subject heading list to a thesaurus we would have to create many relations like

Russia–History EQ Russia+History

But this is only a minor problem: each system has its own way of looking at relations. Many times these relations are only partial or inexact. ISO 25964-2 tries to offer a solution for all cases. But as it is very new there are still no elaborated examples of mappings, and the question remains how a mapping could be done in a way that software will be able to handle it. ISO 25964-2 doesn't answer that question; it only provides a conceptual frame and presents the basic instruments.

In Chapter 12 we will see from another angle that efforts are being made to let different indexing systems talk to each other.

What makes a good indexing system?

Whereas one can find many documents and manuals repeating the same theory about mainly thesauri, there is little to be read about the criteria for evaluating thesauri, let alone subject headings. Maria Pinto, who looked for criteria to evaluate thesauri in social science databases, came to the disappointing conclusion that '[s]pecific literature on the subject of thesaurus quality is almost nonexistent' [22]. She found that four factors play a role in the quality of a thesaurus (in order of importance), each consisting of a few variables:

- The conceptual framework: perceived equivalence relationships, perceived associative relationships, perceived searching options and perceived precoordination levels.

- Performance: all required terms found, perceived explanatory notes, and expected performance.

- Format: perceived thesaurus structure, expected pre-coordination levels, expected ergonomics, and expected display.

- External aids: use of thesaurus structure, use of help elements, and perceived visibility of help systems.

A few years earlier Leslie Ann Owens and Pauline Atherton Cochrane made a distinction between the following kinds of evaluation criteria [23]:

- Structural evaluation: does the vocabulary comply with the standards?

- Formative evaluation: e.g. are synonyms properly controlled?

- Comparative evaluation: is a certain vocabulary better suited for a certain audience than another one?

- Observational evaluation: is it up to the user's expectations?

The article does not give a complete checklist of each of the evaluation methods; it refers to individual studies of vocabularies using one method or the other.

After half a century the theory on how to evaluate a thesaurus, or by extension, a controlled vocabulary, is still in its infancy. For sure, we can assume that the following elements should play a role in such a process:

- Accordance with theory – if any – which will be much easier when evaluating thesauri than subject headings.
- Accordance with the subject(s) covered.
- User-friendliness – a topic that is open for a lot of discussion.
- The level of precoordination.

As we have seen, LCSH follow their own way, sometimes in the opposite direction of well known principles, sometimes giving in to other needs than simple confirmation to the rules. Does this make it a bad system? Obviously not, as the fact that it is the most widely used system in the world may suggest. In her book, Lois Mai Chan sums up the advantages of LCSH [24]:

- LCSH covers all subject areas.
- It offers synonym and homograph control.
- It contains rich links.
- It is a precoordinate system.
- It facilitates browsing of multiple-concept or multifaceted subjects.
- It has been translated and adopted into other systems.

That it is a vast system is true, but that is about the only characteristic which it does not have in common with many others.

What Lois Mai Chan does not say is that the subject headings just come for free as part of the records that so many libraries throughout the world copy daily from the Library of Congress. In the old days they could be found in the 'cataloguing in publication' (CIP) data on the reverse site of the title page of books – and in fact they still are. I have seen university libraries in Africa where this is the main reason for copying them into the catalogue, although the library officially uses a different system, e.g. *Sears List of Subject Headings.*

Hope A. Olson, an authority on cultural and sexual bias in classifications and other library systems, wrote in 2000 about the importance and impact of LCSH [25]: 'Not only is it used in many parts of the world beyond the United States and in languages other than English, but the Library of Congress's application of LCSH is also used worldwide through copy cataloguing. OCLC, for example, has a database containing approximately 42 million bibliographic records of which over 7 million originated with the Library of Congress.'

The discussions among the supporters of thesauri and subject headings are still going on. Gregory Wool has pointed out that a few irrational motives may at least play some role [26]: 'The psychological appeal of greater freedom to craft one's own access strategy combined with an expanded toolbox for data analysis makes postcoordinate features easier to "sell" to the user. In addition, though, developments within librarianship during the 1990s have displayed a weakening of support for precoordinated subject access.'

Meanwhile this discussion is overshadowed by a more fundamental one: is it still necessary – or even wise or feasible – to use controlled vocabulary for indexing? Is it not better – and surely cheaper – to leave indexing to computer systems which can do this automatically? In the next chapter we will look into the arguments of both parties: the supporters and the opponents of automatic indexing.

Notes

1. Examples from the 'Thesaurus of Economic, Social and Cultural Rights'. Available at: *http://shr.aaas.org/thesaurus/*
2. Sometimes terms with only related terms are considered to be orphan terms; sometimes terms with only related terms are allowed.
3. More on the ISIS software family can be found at *http://www. unesco.org/isis*

References

[1] Smith, G. (2008), *Tagging: People-powered Metadata for the Social Web*. Berkeley, CA: New Riders, p. 72.

[2] Tavakolizadeh-Ravari, M. (2007), *Analysis of the Long Term Dynamics in Thesaurus Development and its Consequences*. Berlin: Humboldt-Universität zu Berlin.

[3] Mai Chan, L. (2005), *Library of Congress Subject Headings: Principles and Application*. Englewood, CO: Libraries Unlimited, p. 11.

[4] Stone, A.T. (2000), 'The LCSH century: a brief history of the Library of Congress Subject Headings, and introduction to the centennial essays', *Cataloging & Classification Quarterly*, 29, 1–2: 6.

[5] Cutter, C.A. (2008), *Rules for a Dictionary Catalogue*. Charleston SC: BiblioBazaar.

[6] Bloomfield, M. (2001), 'Indexing: neglected and poorly understood', *Cataloging & Classification Quarterly*, 33, 1: 74.

[7] Broughton, V. (2012), *Essential Library of Congress Subject Headings*. London: Facet Publishing.

[8] National Information Standards Organization (2005), ANSI/NISO Z39.19: 'Guidelines for the construction, format, and management of monolingual controlled vocabularies'. Available from: *http://www.niso.org/kst/ reports/standards?step=2&gid=&project_key=7cc9b58 3cb5a62e8c15d3099e0bb46bbae9cf38a*

[9] Gallagher Tuley, L. (2007), *Thesaurus of Psychological Index Terms*. Washington: American Psychological Association.

[10] International Federation of Library Associations (2005), 'Guidelines for multilingual thesauri'. Available from: *http://archive.ifla.org/VII/s29/pubs/Profrep 115.pdf*

[11] British Standards (2005–7), 'BS 8723: Structured vocabularies for information retrieval' (four parts), Available from: *http://www.standardscentre.co.uk/ search_result.php?search=BS+8723&x=0&y=0*

[12] Wool, G. (2000), 'Filing and precoordination: how subject headings are displayed in online catalogs and why it matters', *Cataloging & Classification Quarterly*, 29, 1–2: 95.

[13] Library of Congress (2007), 'Library of Congress Subject Headings: pre- vs. post-coordination and related issues'. Available from: *http://www.loc.gov/ catdir/cpso/pre_vs_post.pdf*

[14] Mai Chan, L. (2005), *Library of Congress Subject Headings: Principles and Application*. Englewood, CO: Libraries Unlimited, p. 182.

[15] Ibid. p. 96.

[16] Dykstra, M. (1988), 'LC Subject Headings disguised as a thesaurus: something had to be done with LC subject headings, but is this it?', *Library Journal*, 113, 4: 42–6.

[17] Aitchison, J. and Dextre Clarke, S. (2004), 'The thesaurus: a historical viewpoint, with a look to the future', *Cataloging & Classification Quarterly*, 37: 12.

[18] United Nations Educational, Scientific and Cultural Organization. 'The UNESCO Thesaurus'. Available from: *http://databases.unesco.org/thesaurus*

[19] United Nations. 'The UNBIS Thesaurus'. Available from: *http://unhq-appspub-01.un.org/LIB/ DHLUNBISThesaurus.nsf/$$searche?OpenForm*

[20] United Nations Food and Agriculture Organization. 'The AGROVOC Thesaurus'. Available from: *http:// aims.fao.org/standards/agrovoc/functionalities/search*

[21] European Union. 'The EuroVoc Thesaurus'. Available from: *http://eurovoc.europa.eu/drupal/*

[22] Pinto, M. (2008), 'A user view of the factors affecting quality of thesauri in social science databases', *Library & Information Science Research*, 30: 217.

[23] Owens, L.A. and Atherton Cochrane, P. (2004), 'Thesaurus evaluation', *Cataloging & Classification Quarterly*, 37, 3–4: 87–102.

[24] Mai Chan, L. (2005), *Library of Congress Subject Headings: Principles and Application*. Englewood, CO: Libraries Unlimited, p. 408.

[25] Olson, H.A. (2000), 'Difference, culture and change: the untapped potential of LCSH', *Cataloging & Classification Quarterly*, 29, 1–2: 58.

[26] Wool, G. (2000), 'Filing and precoordination: how subject headings are displayed in online catalogs and why it matters', *Cataloging & Classification Quarterly*, 29, 1–2: 100.

2

Automatic indexing versus manual indexing

Machine indexing is rotten and human indexing is capricious.

(Masse Bloomfield [1])

Abstract: This chapter gives an overview of the arguments used in the discussion between the supporters of manual indexing and those of automatic indexing. The arguments against manual indexing are that it is slow, expensive, not detailed enough, that it does not lead to better retrieval, that it is outdated and document centred and that there is no consistency between indexers. The arguments against automatic indexing are that it does not provide an overview of the index terms, that it does not solve the problem of synonyms and variants, that it does not take the context into account, that it does not allow browsing related terms, that orthography may be an impediment and, finally, that it is too complex for computers. The end of the chapter gives an overview of the six most popular misconceptions about automatic indexing.

Key words: manual indexing, automatic indexing.

Introduction

Librarians still consider it to be part of their core business to maintain and apply classifications, subject headings and thesauri. They are trained in library schools to use them, they write about them in journals or discuss them in conferences. In their opinion, books or articles simply cannot be found in a library without their skilled work of indexing. More and more this is no longer self-evident. Even professionals ask if we can afford manual indexing and if we should not devote our time and money to other activities, although their doubts may provoke fierce reactions from colleagues.

The discussion about manual indexing is also one about controlled vocabularies, because manual indexing is normally done by means of thesauri or subject headings. This chapter will give the arguments of defenders and opponents of manual indexing by means of a controlled vocabulary – and, as a consequence, those of the defenders and opponents of automatic indexing, which has been, up to now, still the main alternative. Manual indexing by non-professionals, authors or readers, can also be a competitor to professional indexing. Some aspects of this will also be discussed in this chapter, although Chapter 9, which deals with tagging, will go into more detail.

Arguments against manual indexing

Manual indexing is slow

In his classic book *Everything is Miscellaneous*, David Weinberger describes the daily challenge the cataloguing section in the Library of Congress faces every single day:

> Every *day*, more books come into the library than the 6,487 volumes Thomas Jefferson donated in 1815 to kick-start the collection after the British burned the place down. The incoming books are quickly sorted

into cardboard boxes by topic. The boxes are delivered to three to four hundred catalogers, who between them represent eighty different subject specializations. They examine each book to see which of the library's 285,000 subject headings is most appropriate. Books can be assigned up to ten different subject headings. Keeping America's books non-miscellaneous is a big job [2].

Backlogs in libraries not always are the result of the overwhelming amount of new arrivals in the cataloguing section; they may be due to many other factors: limited budgets, which can cause understaffing, time-consuming cataloguing practices, etc. Indexing can indeed play a role in this too. It takes at least a few minutes for a cataloguer to find out what the exact subject of a book is and which thesaurus terms are the best translation of that subject. If a cataloguer needs five minutes to index a publication and another 15 to create a new catalogue record, he could save a quarter of his time if indexing terms were added automatically. These kinds of calculations may be appealing, especially to managers, when budgets are cut down.

Manual indexing is expensive

Because of the amount of time it takes to find suitable indexing terms, indexing will cost a lot of money. The only way to make it cheaper – or even affordable in some cases – is to outsource it to countries where highly trained professionals do the work for substantially lower wages. A simple search for 'outsourcing indexing India' in Google will reveal all kinds of firms who offer these (and other) services. Of course, this will only be an alternative in English-speaking countries.

But it is also expensive to create, update and learn a controlled vocabulary. It can take years for a team of librarians and specialists to create a good thesaurus. At least one colleague must devote part of his or her time to updating the thesaurus and he or she will have to consult other colleagues or specialists from time to time to ask for their advice. New colleagues will need up to six months to get fully acquainted with the controlled vocabulary.

In a report, commissioned in 2006 by the Library of Congress, Karen Calhoun made many suggestions to reduce costs. One of them was: 'Abandon the attempt to do comprehensive subject analysis manually with LCSH in favour of subject keywords; urge LC to dismantle LCSH' [3]. This suggestion has raised many protests from the library world. Abandoning LCSH would lead to 'scholarly catastrophe' and 'bibliobarbarism' [4]. Of course, Thomas Mann (not the German writer, but the researcher at the Library of Congress), who is a defender of traditional indexing systems like the Library of Congress Subject Headings, does not agree with Calhoun's views. In a critical review of her report [5] he argues against replacing controlled vocabulary with keywords. His arguments are:

- A controlled vocabulary leads to a whole variety of titles that could not be found using only keywords.
- Browsing through the LCSH terms 'brings aspects of the subject to the attention of researchers that they would not think, beforehand, even to exist'.

In the end, Calhoun's argument is that we can do with less, but with still enough quality, if we want to reduce the costs; Mann's point is that quality is paramount, whatever the cost may be.

Manual indexing is not detailed enough

Because indexing is expensive and slow, libraries mostly have a policy of global indexing. This means that a book containing

42

essays on ten twentieth-century writers will only get one indexing term; it will be treated as a book on twentieth-century literature. A reader interested in one out of the ten novelists must be clever enough to go through the books indexed as 'English literature–Twentieth century' too.

The Library of Congress has several rules that apply to cases where more than one subject is treated in a book. They are called the 'rule of three' and the 'rule of four'. The 'rule of three' stipulates the following: 'For a work covering two or three topics treated separately, a heading representing precisely each of the topics is assigned. The two or three specific headings are assigned in favor of a general heading if the latter includes in its scope more than three subtopics' [6].

The 'rule of four' is applied in cases 'when the work being cataloged deals with four topics, each of which forms only a small portion of a general topic' [7]. For such a work four headings may be assigned, but in other cases a work with four topics may get a more general heading; five is always one too many. If you are a secondary school pupil who has to write an essay on an author, you not only should know that you must look under a more general subject too, but also that you must consult a specialized database in order to find all (chapters of) books in the library dealing with your author. This may be asking too much from someone who is not an experienced researcher, and as a consequence the library probably does not fulfil the needs of the most interested public for this kind of literature.

Manual indexing does not necessarily lead to better retrieval

Some research has been conducted in order to find out if manual indexing increases search results. At least in library catalogues, indexing leads to better retrieval: more than

30 per cent of the records cannot be found if only keywords and no descriptors are used in the search [8]. The authors of these studies recognize that adding tables of content to the catalogue records creates a new situation, for which their conclusions must be re-examined, but they do not tell anything about the effects on retrieval when controlled vocabulary terms are added to full text documents, where every word can be used as a search term. Other research pointed out that adding subject heading to fiction does not increase circulation, at least not in academic libraries [9]. Comparing searches based on automatic text-word indexing or manually assigned controlled descriptors, J. Savoy found that the searches in an abstract database using controlled descriptors were slightly better, but the differences were statistically insignificant. The best results were obtained using a combination of keywords and controlled vocabulary terms [10]. As a consequence he makes a suggestion that might be very tempting for database producers: 'From the point of view of bibliographic database developers, a single automatic indexing procedure that is clearly faster and cheaper might be adopted' [10: 888].

Other researchers found that controlled vocabulary terms can improve recall and precision if the searcher uses thesaurus terms from records he gets as a result of a search based on keywords [11].

The American National Library of Medicine has built a 'Metathesaurus' of about 150 (English) controlled vocabularies [12]. But such an instrument may be exceptional; normally, someone who is consulting more than one catalogue or database must find out how their subject is indexed in each one of them.

This may also have consequences for constructing union catalogues or conducting corporate searches, i.e. searches by means of software that can repeat one search in many databases in one go. The database vendor EBSCOHost has many databases with and without a thesaurus. The interface makes it possible to search through more than one database with a single search command, but as the user chooses two or more databases with a thesaurus, the thesaurus search option disappears because of the incompatibility between them.

Nowadays federated search applications are considered a solution in situations where researchers are confronted with a multitude of databases. These programmes offer a single search interface and launch a search into up to ten databases in one run. In their advanced search options the user can limit his search to one particular field, e.g. the 'author' field. If he or she chooses the 'subject' field, the search is executed through all the fields that have something to do with subject indexing: keywords, subject headings, thesaurus terms, author-assigned keywords, etc.

These two examples illustrate that the advantages of manual indexing may disappear in a modern search environment where many databases are at the disposal of the searcher by means of a single interface. It then is no longer possible to rely on the knowledge that a manual-assigned subject heading or thesaurus term normally increases the precision of the search.

Controlled vocabularies are outdated

Controlled vocabularies cannot catch up with the fast changing modern world. It takes too much time and effort to update them. New terms may take months, or even years, to get approved of by a team of (expensive) experts. This is not an appealing prospect to managers of information services who run tight budgets. Thesauri enjoy more tolerance than subject headings, which are sometimes despised as being instruments dating from the pre-computer era.

Controlled vocabularies are document centred

Controlled vocabularies try to summarize the subject of a text in one or a few words; they do not express what this text means for a particular reader. They are superficial; they only try to say what the text is about (i.e. they deal with the *aboutness* or *ofness*). Probably more important is the *meaning* of the text: what does it say about the subject? Another argument against controlled vocabularies is that they cannot express the importance of a text for the reader's life, the *relevance* of it. The aboutness of a book on dogs is *dogs*; the meaning can be that it is nice to have a dog as a pet, but that you need to invest a lot of time in training the animal if you want to enjoy it as a pet. For one reader the relevance of this book will be that he wants to buy a dog and train it. Another reader will conclude that he has no time to keep a dog. A third reader will not believe the author, since he has a nice little dog which does not take all that much of his time.

Even if we take it for granted that controlled vocabularies only express the aboutness, there is still a problem. For a lung cancer specialist, the aboutness of an article is not 'lung cancer' because he only reads articles related to that subject. He wants to know if an article gives information about a particular treatment and even more: does it discuss advantages or disadvantages of the treatment; does it contain new developments in the treatment, etc.? In 1988 Bella Hass Weinberg published a now classic article with the suggestive title 'Why indexing fails the researcher' [13] in which she opposed aboutness (or topic) to aspect (or comment). 'It is contended', she writes, 'that the scholar/researcher is primarily interested in comment, and an index limited to identifying the literature about a topic, with only broad subcategorization, is next to useless for the scholar's purpose.' To illustrate her view she applies this to her own experiences in writing the article:

> The thesis of this paper was supported in the process of its preparation – it took five times as long to retrieve the references to document the ideas that the author recalled having heard or read as it did to write the paper. Presumably, a search to determine whether any of the ideas believed to be new in this paper had ever been expressed before in the literature would take many years, requiring a sequential reading of the library-information science literature, rather than the consulting of indexes.

Indexers do not agree with each other nor with themselves . . .

Among information professionals it is a platitude that two indexers add different descriptors to the same document and that the same indexer would not index a document the way he or she used to six months before. Studies about inter-indexer consistency have been going on for more than half a century now[1] with a climax in the 1960s, the 'golden age of consistency studies', as Olson and Wolfram call them [14]. And, although the topic may not be as hot as it was then, each year new publications are added to the already long list.

The results in these studies range from 10 per cent to 80 per cent, suggesting that the result of indexing with controlled vocabularies is not that much controlled at all. Recent studies even seem to emphasize that tagging, i.e. 'in essence, indexing by nonprofessionals without the benefit of a controlled vocabulary' [15] is more consistent than professional indexing.

Is indexing by the author or editor a valuable alternative?

If manual indexing by indexers is not such a great idea, and if we do not want to wait for an anonymous and uncontrollable army of social taggers to take care of the job, maybe we should leave it to the authors themselves? This ensures a number of advantages:

- Authors know best what their texts are about and what their meaning or relevance could be.

- They are experts in their field; they know all the details and do not have to invest extra time in finding relevant indexing terms.

- The costs are low: authors can add indexing terms to their text while writing it. We do not have to pay a second person to do so.

Research about the usefulness of keywords added by authors to their own texts has revealed the following [16]. Adding keywords to the text itself is not common practice in all disciplines. It varies from 5 per cent in arts to 50 per cent in medicine and 75 per cent in statistics. Editors have different methods for supplying keywords:

- Authors can add keywords to their text with no restrictions.

- Authors can add a limited number of keywords.

- Authors have to choose from a list.

In some journals not the authors but the editors or their referees supply the keywords. They too can use different methods:

- They may add the keywords they consider appropriate.

- They may change and supplement the authors' keywords.

- They may choose keywords from a list.

- Or they may supply keywords according to rules applied for all the editor's journals or just for that one journal.

There is no guarantee that authors or editors are doing a better job than professional indexers:

- Sometimes they do not pay enough attention to the keywords; it's just one of those things they have to do after finishing the article.

- They may try to claim a wider audience or situate their text in the field of popular research topics by supplying keywords which go beyond the range of the content of the text.

- The keywords may be too personal or too vague.

Other research found that bibliographic databases added descriptors that in 25 per cent of the cases were exactly the same as the authors' keywords, and in 21 per cent a normalized version of them. Gil-Leiva and Alonso-Arroyo were rather optimistic about their research and concluded that 'keywords provided by authors are a valuable source of information for both human indexing and for automatic indexing systems of journal articles' [17]. One could also argue that for more than 50 per cent of the articles indexers did not agree with the keywords the authors provided, and that in another 20 per cent these keywords gave them only a vague idea which descriptor to choose. C. Rockelle Strader compared author-assigned keywords to LCSH in a catalogue of electronic theses and dissertations, a kind of database for which it is common that authors fill in the metadata and add keywords [18]. His findings were that 44.49 per cent of the author-assigned keywords did not match cataloguer-assigned LCSH. He has different explanations for this:

- LCSH does not keep up with current research and consequently the author has to invent his or her own keywords.

- The author may have been inspired by keywords assigned in databases of articles or chapters, which are not used as a source for new controlled terms in LCSH. In other words: author-assigned keywords and LCSH come from a different world.

- The author-assigned keywords may be variations of LCSH.

- Some keywords do not express the topic of the document, but e.g. the degree for which the thesis was written.

- Other keywords were an attempt to formulate the author's opinion about the meaning or the relevance of the work at hand.

Strader is also optimistic as to the quality of author-assigned keywords: 'The data gathered in this study suggest that authors performed rather effectively (when compared to assigned LCSH) in providing relevant keywords. A total of 65.44 per cent of author-assigned keywords matched exactly, partially matched, or were variant forms of LCSH' [18: 249]. The question remains as to what this means in view of retrieval, and especially in terms of precision, recall and noise (Strader notes that one author assigned 57 keywords).

In Chapter 9, on tagging, we will have to come back to the issue of controlled vocabularies assigned by professionals compared to keywords assigned by (cheaper) third parties. The baseline in this discussion will also be that if keywords provided by non-professionals are good enough, we can do without the professionals. But first, let us look at the arguments of the supporters of manual indexing.

Arguments in favour of manual indexing

In recent years defenders of manual indexing must have found a lot of support in the writings of Thomas Mann. He published several articles to explain why automatic and full text indexing cannot beat traditional library work [19, 20, 21, 22]. His and other people's arguments are:

Automatic indexing does not provide a coherent overview of index terms

Full text indexing results in a chaotic mass of search terms, whereas structured vocabularies provide lists of controlled terms to browse. A researcher who uses a library catalogue can browse through those lists and explore the various combinations of terms. Each of those terms stands for one or more texts which were conscientiously selected and indexed by the library. Someone who uses a search engine like Google will be confronted with hundreds of thousands and even millions of hits referring to web pages of dubious quality, which only have in common that the keyword entered in the search box is one of many words in them.

Thomas Mann compares the search for the history of Afghanistan in Google with browsing through the subject headings in a library OPAC starting from 'Afghanistan'. Google will give you more than 11 000 000 hits, of which the highest ranked may only be good enough to be used in high school. Librarian-created subject headings give a systematic overview of all related subdivisions of each subject. What Thomas Mann does not mention is that this may well be the case for a precoordinative indexing system like subject headings, which allows browsing through a whole list of subjects starting with the word 'Afghanistan', but not for postcoordinative systems in which the user has to think of descriptors he can combine with 'Afghanistan'. The searcher's inspiration may be limited to 'Afghanistan AND history' and in this way he will miss some unpredictable combinations like 'Afghanistan AND Historiography' or 'Afghanistan AND Kings AND Rulers'.

Automatic indexing does not solve the problems of synonyms or variants

Controlled vocabularies make a distinction between preferred and non-preferred terms. Among all possible synonyms a choice is made in favour of that term which is the best expression of the idea behind it: the preferred term. All other synonyms relate to that term. Automatic indexing results in a pile of words without any kind of relation between them. Morphological and semantic variants are ignored. Moreover, if words are extracted from a text by automatic indexing, they will be in the language of the text. This means that we are obliged to use search terms in as many languages as we know in order to find enough texts that were written in them. Controlled vocabularies, on the other hand, are excellent instruments in a multilingual situation: they confront the user with only one language.

In an article with the obvious title, 'The weakness of full-text searching', Jeffrey Beall gives quite a long list of language variations and other problems which lead to loss of information in automatic indexing [23], among which are:

■ Synonyms.

■ Variant spellings, e.g. differences between British and American English, or modern spelling and the spelling of a few centuries ago.

Automatic indexing versus manual indexing

- Shortened forms of terms: abbreviations, acronyms, initialisms.
- Different languages or dialects.
- Obsolete terms.
- The greater degree of variation in terminology in the humanities.
- The homonym problem, i.e. a word or phrase with more than one meaning.
- True homonyms, i.e. words with two or more meanings.
- Lack of disambiguation of personal names.
- False cognates, i.e. words which are spelled (almost) the same in two languages, but which have a different meaning.
- Inability to search by facets: all words are on an equal level; there is no way to tell if they refer to a place, a time, a format, etc.
- The aboutness problem, which is of another nature than the aboutness problem in indexing with controlled vocabularies. In full text indexing it is even not easy to tell what the text is about.
- Figurative language.
- Word lists: scanned dictionaries and all kinds of lists may come up as a result of a search in a full-text environment like Google Books because they contain the search term.
- Abstract topics: a search for 'free will' will generate an enormous amount of texts and maybe only a few dealing with it as a philosophical topic.
- The incognito problem: the subject is not mentioned directly.
- Search term not in resource: an article on soccer may not contain the word 'soccer' because it is all too obvious to the reader that this is the subject.

His conclusion is: 'Over the past fifteen years, most information retrieval has transitioned from searching based on rich metadata to full-text searching. The result of this transition is an overall decrease in the quality of information retrieval' [23: 444].

Automatic indexing does not take the context into account

There is no guarantee as to the quality of the documents retrieved by a Google search: texts written by scholars are listed next to all kinds of rubbish. But even in databases of scientific publications a search based on full text indexing gives a lot of irrelevant answers. Words that are only used casually are not distinguishable from those which are related to the subject of the paper. A study by Shah *et al.* [24] showed that the part of an article from which a keyword is taken is relevant. The best keywords are in the Abstract, followed by the Introduction. Keywords from Methods, Results and Discussion are not very accurate. This is not surprising: in Methods the author discusses which techniques he used in his experiment. He will probably compare his investigation to those of other researchers who used the same method on different subjects. If he is writing an article on breast cancer he might compare his methods to others who used it to study stomach, lung or liver cancers and produce sentences like: 'Author X applied this method to study lung cancer, etc.' A search for 'lung' adjacent to 'cancer' will find this article, although it does not discuss lung cancer at all. The same goes for the Results and Discussion part, where the results are discussed in view of other scientific work in the same or related fields.

Of course the argument of the opponents of automatic indexing is that it does not distinguish between the different parts of an article.

Automatic indexing does not allow browsing related subjects

Libraries use classification schemes to order documents. These produce a systematic classification of documents which are similar or which differ only slightly from each other. A researcher can browse the stacks (or an electronic version) and make discoveries which are not possible in the way in which electronic documents are ordered nowadays. Moreover, a search engine confronts us with so many thousands of results that we quickly lose all courage to browse them.

Thomas Mann gives the following example: he was once looking for the title of the first book published in French and couldn't find the answer in Google. He then went to the bookshelves hoping to find a certain catalogue of French books, which was missing; the book next to its empty place on the shelf attracted his attention. He took it from the shelf and found in it the information he was looking for [21].

Orthography is an impediment to automatic indexing

Computer technology has a short history and orthography a very long one. One of the consequences is that spelling has no consideration for the limitations of computer programmes. The result may be that many meaningful words and entities are chopped up into meaningless parts, e.g.

- Names like O'Brian are cut up into 'O' and 'Brian'; 'Van Dam' into 'Van' and 'Dam', etc.
- Alzheimer's Disease will become Alzheimer s Disease.
- P&O becomes P O.
- 9/11 becomes 9 11; 2000 will end up as 2 and 000.

- MS-DOS is indexed as MS and DOS, and CD-ROM as CD and ROM.

Brooks (1998) has checked those and similar cases in three influential database vendor systems and concluded that they had an 'ad hoc, arbitrary treatment of language' [25]. As more and more non-academic material is indexed, spelling errors, typos and sloppy spelling is becoming a huge problem. Proctor states: 'While it may be true that "no-one" (or, at least, no intelligent, educated, adult native speaker) is likely to be misled by such carelessness, the vast majority of search engines, optical character recognition (OCR) software, and speech synthesizers will be' [26].

Typos and spelling errors were also a problem in the days when full text material was restricted to paper and databases only contained bibliographic references of it.[2] For full text indexing it has become a bigger problem because of a few new phenomena [27]:

- Authors publish their own texts in repositories and electronic journals, which are not always peer reviewed as paper journals used to be. Also, these texts are no longer checked by professional correctors and editors.

- Printed texts are scanned and read by OCR software. Although OCR techniques have made enormous progress in the last decades, they are still not perfect. As more and more large quantities of texts are scanned it is impossible to control the output by human experts. Nearly every repository of scanned texts will contain errors like 'tbeory' (for 'theory') and 'tbat' (for 'that') or 'offical' (for 'official').

- Digital texts are converted from one format into another, e.g. from a word processor text into PDF or from PDF into HTML. In the process of conversion, errors may slip in.

Indexing is too complex for computers

The results of automatic indexing are of lesser quality than those of manual indexing and the techniques may only be applicable to some sorts of texts. Even professional indexers do not trust indexing programmes; they do not rely on automatic indexing, but on 'computer aided indexing'. Lancaster (1998) ends his chapter on automatic indexing with this conclusion: 'While some progress has been made in applying computers to various tasks related to information retrieval, little evidence exists that automatic procedures can yet outperform humans in such intellectual tasks as indexing, abstracting, thesaurus construction, and the creation of search strategies' [28].

This is also the view of Jeffrey Garrett in his article 'KWIC and Dirty?' [29] (with a nod to the KWIC (Keyword in Context) technique – which in fact has nothing to do with automatic or full-text indexing, but all the more with displaying terms in a printed thesaurus). Garrett 'points to certain disjunctions between the machine processes that enable full-text searching and the subtle cognitive processes that underlie human learning and reasoning.'

Some misconceptions about automatic indexing

Automatic indexing = full text indexing

Full text indexing means that every word of a text is indexed and consequently retrievable. In most cases stop words like 'the', 'a' or 'with' are not included. Of course, this can only be done automatically because it would be too expensive and time consuming to do it manually. Full text indexing is comparable to book indexing, which has been a common practice for scientific books since the nineteenth century, but goes back as far as the sixteenth century. Until the 1980s, book indexes were merely constructed manually. For classical Latin texts and Bible texts, indexes were published that are as detailed as automatically produced full text indexes. This means that it is possible to make full text indexes manually – although it might be far too expensive to do so.

On the other hand, automatic indexing does not have to lead to full text indexes and it does not have to be executed upon the text itself. Automatic indexing can produce abstracts or a single subject term. It can also act upon a representation of the text, be it a bibliographic description or an abstract.

Automatic indexing = uncontrolled indexing

It is not necessarily true that automatic indexing extracts all words from the texts in the exact morphological form in which they appear in the text. A number of techniques are developed to transform them to more controlled terms.

Automatic indexing = natural language indexing

Natural language indexing is opposed to indexing with controlled vocabularies, e.g. thesauri, or classification codes. Automatic indexing programmes can compare index terms with controlled vocabularies or classifications and retrieve index terms from them.

Automatic indexing = every word is equal

Of course, it is possible to extract each word from a text and treat it as equal, but normally this is not what happens.

Many systems disregard words with little or no meaning, stop words like 'the' or 'in' or 'for'. More complex systems calculate the information value of each word compared to all words in the texts or a given set of texts.

Automatic indexing cannot handle scientific formulae

This is no longer the case: it is possible to index e.g. chemical formulae.

Automatic indexing is only possible for text material

Of course texts are much easier to index automatically than music, photos or films, but it is possible to index these materials too. In the last decade intensive research in this area was executed and the first results are available now. Some of them can be seen freely on the Internet, as we will explain in Chapters 4, 5 and 6.

Conclusion

This chapter began with objections that can be made against manual indexing and ended with some misconceptions about automatic indexing. Here and there we learned that even indexing as such is not without fundamental problems and that author-assigned keywords are only a partial alternative for professional indexing. Later on we will be confronted with the question whether other cheaper indexers, i.e. the vast army of benevolent taggers, can bring any solace or not. We will also see to what extent the opponents of automatic and full-text indexing of our present-day most prominent source of text materials, the web, are right when they claim that Google, as the most dominant search engine, just extracts words from texts and presents them to us in bulk.

In the next chapter we will first describe some basic techniques used in automatic text indexing.

Notes

1. In 1977 Lawrence E. Leonard made a summary of inter-indexer consistency studies from the mid-1950s up to then in 'Inter-indexer consistency studies, 1954–1975: a review of the literature and summary of study results'. Available at: *http://www.ideals.illinois.edu/bitstream/handle/2142/3885/gslisoccasionalpv00000i00131.pdf?sequence=1*
2. Lists of common typos, the so-called dirty database lists, were made by librarians in order to check their catalogues for typos (see e.g. *http://www.terryballard.org/typos/typoscomplete.html*).

References

[1] Bloomfield, M. (2002), 'Indexing: neglected and poorly understood', *Cataloging & Classification Quarterly*, 33, 1: 63–75.

[2] Weinberger, D. (2007), *Everything is Miscellaneous: the Power of the New Digital Disorder*. New York: Holt, p. 15.

[3] Calhoun, K. (2006), 'The changing nature of the catalog and its integration with other discovery tools'. Available from: *http://www.loc.gov/catdir/calhoun-report-final.pdf*

[4] Oder, N. (2006), 'The end of LC Subject Headings?', *Library Journal*, 131, 9: 14–15.

[5] Mann, T. (2008), 'The Changing nature of the catalog and its integration with other discovery tools: final report, March 17, 2006; prepared for the Library of Congress by Karen Calhoun: a critical review', *Journal of Library Metadata*, 8: 169–97.

[6] Mai Chan, L. (2005), *Library of Congress Subject Headings: Principles and Application*. Englewood, CO: Libraries Unlimited, p. 188.

[7] Ibid. p. 189.

[8] Voorbij, H. (1998), 'Title keywords and subject descriptors: a comparison of subject search entries of books in the humanities and social sciences', *Journal of Documentation*, 54: 466–76.

[9] Wilson, M.D., Spillane, J.L., Cook, C. and Highsmith, A.L. (2000), 'The relationship between subject headings for works of fiction and circulation in an academic library', *Library Collections, Acquisitions & Technical Services*, 24: 459–65.

[10] Savoy, J. (2004), 'Bibliographic database access using free-text and controlled vocabulary: an evaluation', *Information Processing and Management*, 41: 873–90.

[11] IJzereef, L., Kamps, J. and De Rijke, M. 'Biomedical retrieval: how can a thesaurus help?', in Meersman, R. and Tari, Z. (eds) (2005), *On the Move to Meaningful Internet Systems 2005: CoopIS, DOA and ODBASE*, Heidelberg: Springer Berlin, pp. 1432–48.

[12] The American National Library of Medicine. *http://www.nlm.nih.gov/pubs/factsheets/umlsmeta.html*

[13] Weinberg, B.H. (1988), 'Why indexing fails the researcher', *The Indexer*, 16: 3–6.

[14] Olson, H.A. and Wolfram, D. (2006), 'Indexing consistency and its implications for information architecture: a pilot study'. Available from: *http://iasummit.org/2006/files/175_Presentation_Desc.pdf*

[15] Wolfram, D., Olson, H.A. and Bloom, R. (2009), 'Measuring consistency for multiple taggers using Vector Space Modeling', *Journal of the American Society for Information Science and Technology*, 60: 1997.

[16] Hartley, J. and Kostoff, R.N. (2003), 'How useful are "keywords" in scientific journals?', *Journal of Information Science*, 29: 433–8.

[17] Gil-Leiva, I. and Alonso-Arroyo, A. (2007) 'Keywords given by authors of scientific articles in database descriptors', *Journal of the American Society for Information Science and Technology*, 58: 1175–87.

[18] Rockelle Strader, C. (2009), 'Author-assigned keywords versus Library of Congress Subject Headings: implications for the cataloging of electronic theses and dissertations', *Library Resources & Technical Services*, 53: 243–50.

[19] Mann, T. (2005), 'Google Print vs. onsite collections', *American libraries*, 36, 7: 45–6.

[20] Mann, T. (2005) 'Research at risk: when we undermine cataloging, we undermine scholarship', *Library Journal*, July 2005. Available from: *http://www.libraryjournal.com/article/CA623006.html*

[21] Mann, T. (2005), 'Will Google's keyword searching eliminate the need for LC cataloging and classification?' Available from *http://www.guild2910.org/searching.htm*

[22] Mann, T. (2008), 'Will Google's keyword searching eliminate the need for LC cataloging and classification?', *Journal of Library Metadata*, 8: 159–68.

[23] Beall, J. (2008), 'The weakness of full-text indexing', *The Journal of Academic Librarianship*, 34: 438–44.

[24] Shah, P.K., Perez-Iratxeta, C., Bork, P. and Andrade, M.A. (2003), 'Information extraction from full text

scientific articles: where are the keywords?', *BMC Bioinformatics*, 29 May 2003; 4: 20.

[25] Brooks, T.A. (1998), 'Orthography as a fundamental impediment to online information retrieval', *Journal of the American Society for Information Science*, 49: 731–41.

[26] Proctor, E. (2002), 'Spelling and searching the Internet: an overlooked problem', *The Journal of Academic Librarianship*, 28, 5: 297–305.

[27] Beall, J. (2005), 'Metadata and data quality problems in the digital library', in: *Journal of Digital Information*, 6, 3: 355.

[28] Lancaster, F.W. (1998), *Indexing and Abstracting in Theory and Practice*. London: Library Association Publishing, p. 296.

[29] Garrett, J. (2006), 'KWIC and dirty?: human cognition and the claim of full-text searching', *Journal of Electronic Publishing*, 9, 1. Available from: *http://dx.doi.org/10.3998/3336451.0009.106*

3

Techniques applied in automatic indexing of text material

Abstract: Automatic indexing of text material can be very basic, or it can involve some advanced techniques. It normally begins with lexical analysis and it can imply the use of stop word lists, stemming techniques, the extraction of meaningful word combinations or statistical term weighting. Sometimes word combinations are linked to controlled vocabularies or classifications. For two decades now the Text REtrieval Conferences (TREC) have been the laboratory for specialists in this field.

Key words: automatic text indexing, stemming, TREC conferences.

Introduction

We are all familiar with automatic indexing of texts because web search engines offer us the possibility to search for every (or almost every) word in web pages, but automatic text indexing is much more than that. In this day and age we find it quite basic that databases of scientific literature offer us the possibility to search through the full text, not only of new articles, which were written by means of word processors, but also of older publications, which originally were written by hand, typed on a typewriter and printed in paper journals. Huge amounts of these texts and all other kinds of publications are scanned and put into the databases of cultural heritage projects.

Although one can compile such a database with a $50 scanner and a freeware OCR programme, a lot of research has been going on in order to get better and more advanced results than just making every word retrievable. Not all of the literature by far on this subject is comprehensible to 'non-techies' – in fact most of it is written by engineers with solid mathematical backgrounds. A good and not too technical introduction may be the book of Marie-Francine Moens, *Automatic Indexing and Abstracting of Document Texts* [1], although it dates from the year 2000 and thus not taking account of the most recent developments.

In this chapter we will only give an overview of the most elementary techniques.

Lexical analysis

Although indexing a text seems a simple problem, it is not. One would think that a programme which takes each word out of the text, i.e. each string of characters between spaces or between spaces and punctuation marks, cannot go wrong. Not only spelling and orthography may cause problems, but also the presence of numbers. If they are ignored as being not meaningful, important information is omitted in economic or scientific texts.

Lexical analysis can go together with techniques for text normalization which convert variants and unusual text elements into 'normal' text, for example:

- correction of spelling errors, probably caused during scanning;
- conversion of upper case to lower case;
- removal of diacritics;
- normalization of abbreviations;
- conversion of numbers into words.

The use of stop word lists

Stop words are (small) words that are not taken into account in the indexing process because they are supposed to be meaningless. Several categories of words can be considered to be stop words:

- Words with only a grammatical function: articles ('the', 'a', 'an'), prepositions ('for', 'in', 'to', 'under', 'by', etc).
- Words that necessarily have a high frequency in a text and by consequence a very low use in retrieval. It is pointless to search for 'computer' in a database on ICT, unless you want to retrieve more than 90% of the records.
- Short words. In general, short words express basic functions in (Western) languages and are basic verbs, prepositions, etc.: 'a', 'the', 'in' in English; 'un', 'le', 'du', 'à' in French or 'ein', 'am', 'um' in German. This of course can be a risky assumption because in scientific literature certain short words are very meaningful, e.g. 'vitamin A'.
- Words with a very low frequency in a text are probably also not very essential to the text.

Some of these lists can be set up beforehand, others can only be built as the database grows.

One of the largest full-text newspaper archives in the world, LexisNexis, uses this stop word list – which it calls its 'noise words' [2]:

the

and

of

his

my

when

there

is

are

so

or

it

In this list 'in' is missing: it is not considered to be a 'noise word' because this would make searches like 'one in a million' impossible.

Indeed, making a solid stop word list is not as self-evident as it seems. A Dutch stop word list would probably contain prepositions like 'van' (English 'of' or 'from') and 'in' (English 'in'), but this would have as a consequence that the name of one of the most important school book publishers in Flanders, *Van In*, is not retrievable.

Stemming

A rudimentary full-text indexing would result in a list of words as they appear in a text. This would be a long list with a substantial amount of words that are very close to each other:

- Singular and plural form of nouns.

- Infinitives and conjugated verbs.

- Nouns and adjectives based on them.

- Etc.

By reducing all these words to their stem the list can be shortened and retrieval can be improved, because now the searcher does not need to consider all possible forms of every word he or she uses. A first technique consists in comparing each word with a list of accepted stems. Only these are then used for the index.

Another method is known as 'stemming' or 'Porter stemming', after the famous 1980 article by M.F. Porter [3]. Prefixes and suffixes are stripped away and each word is reduced to its stem. In this way 'talking' is reduced to 'talk' and 'walked' to 'walk', etc. Many modifications of and alternatives to this method were published during the last quarter of the twentieth century. Some of them relied on statistics to calculate the frequency of certain characters at the beginning or the end of a word; the characters that are the most frequent suggest that this word must be an inflected form of another word, e.g. 's' would suggest a word in plural, etc.

Not all full-text databases use stemming techniques and hence searchers must still learn basic retrieval methods like truncation in order to optimize their recall. This means that they have to enter something like 'vehicle*' or 'vehicle?' If they want to be sure they retrieve 'vehicles' as well as 'vehicle'. When stemming is standard, the opposite is true: the searchers must apply certain techniques if they do not want to retrieve every possible form of the word. Nowadays the Google search engine applies stemming and the Google manual teaches its users how to undo it:

> The query [*http://www.google.com/search?q=child+bic ycle+helmet*] finds pages that contain words that are similar to some or all of your search terms, e.g., 'child,' 'children,' or 'children's,' 'bicycle,' 'bicycles,' 'bicycle's,' 'bicycling,' or 'bicyclists,' and 'helmet' or 'helmets.' Google calls this feature *word variations* or *automatic stemming*. Stemming is a technique to search on the stem or root of a word that can have multiple endings.
>
> If you only want to search for pages that contain some term(s) exactly, precede each such term with a plus sign (+) [*http://www.googleguide.com/plus_operator. html#disableAutomaticStemming*] or enclose more than one term in quotes (' ') [*http://www.googleguide.com/ quoted_phrases.html#exactMatching*] [4].

Some languages, e.g. German, Dutch, Scandinavian languages, have many compound words that are written as one. The English equivalents are mostly written as two words. Stemming does not extract the two building blocks of compound words. Techniques that can break them up are called 'decompounding'; they have had some interest from German researchers [5].

Extracting meaningful word combinations

It is not enough to list all words from a text, and especially in the English language two words next to each other may form one concept. Let's take this now-classical example by James Anderson and José Pérez-Carballo [6]: 'One approach that has been tried in some automatic indexing situations could be a 'try everything' method.' This sentence can be analysed into the following pairs of words:

one approach

approach that

that has

has been

been tried

tried in

in some

some automatic

automatic indexing

indexing situations

situations could

could be

be called

called a

a 'try'

'try everything'

'everything' method

Only the combination 'automatic indexing' can be accepted as a meaningful combination of words.

The list of possible combinations could be matched against a standard list; in this case only 'automatic indexing' will appear in it. Another, less reliable, method consists of comparing word combinations throughout the entire text: if they are found many times, they must be meaningful. A third method checks whether a grammatical relation exists between two or more words. This results in possible meaningful combinations that will be matched against possible variations in the text.

Proper nouns are a special case because they are relatively easy to spot: they can be matched against a list or they can be recognized by the simple fact that each part begins with a capital, and as that capital is not the first character of the sentence, it should be a signal of something else. In some languages many proper names have special words or word combinations. The Dutch 'vander' must be part of a name since in a normal sentence 'van' and 'der' are two separate words. Other examples are:

- words beginning with 'Mc';
- combinations of words of which the first part is a capital followed by a full stop: 'G.', 'T.' etc.;
- articles or prepositions from other languages, e.g. 'van', 'von', 'del', 'de la' in an English text.

Index term weighting

It is not enough to extract terms from a text; we must also evaluate the information value they have. Therefore it is necessary to see every term in the light of all terms in one text and in a corpus of related texts. It is obvious that a text about computers will contain many times such words as 'computer', 'PC', 'IT', 'software', 'hardware', etc. A human indexer would not list 'computer' with all the pages it occurs on in the index at the back of such a book; he or she would have to mention almost every page number.

During the last quarter of a century many formulae have been invented to measure the value of terms in texts. They take into account the following parameters:

- the number of times the term occurs in the text;
- the length of the text;
- the relation of the text to other terms;
- the value of the term in similar and in different texts.

Although all studies on automatic text indexing involve a lot of mathematics, the basic ideas may originate from common sense. Take for instance the 'inverse term frequency', a very popular and one of the oldest formulae. It starts from the frequency of a term in a certain text. This result is compared to the frequency of the term in the whole corpus, i.e. the collections of texts to which it belongs. If the frequency of the term in the text is higher than the one of the term in the corpus, it must be significant for that text. The rest is a matter of putting this reasoning into a good formula, with some logarithms, etc.

Linking words and word combinations to a controlled vocabulary

When we read a text that contains a certain number of words which all express some aspect of a subject or when the text contains certain word combinations, we conclude that this text is about this or that subject. It would be great if an automatic system could do the same thing, especially when large numbers of texts have to be processed.

Each day about 2500 articles are submitted to the Medline database, and it is estimated that by 2015 as many as 1 million articles will be added to the database each year. For some years now methods have been developed to facilitate the indexing of this number of texts [7]. In fact the problem does not lie in the indexing of each word of the articles but in the indexing of the titles and abstracts according to a controlled vocabulary, the Medical Subject Headings (MeSH).

As a subject heading system, MeSH consists of terms which can have one or more subdivisions. It also contains a set of rules that determine which subdivision is allowed for which term. This is especially tricky in MeSH. That is the reason why much of the literature concentrates on this problem. The methods involve statistical techniques to determine which of the possible subdivisions is best suited for a certain publication, but the results are such that we can only speak of 'computer-aided indexing'. A human indexer has to accept or reject the suggestions the system makes. Névéol *et al.* see advantages and disadvantages for the indexers:

> The recommendation of relevant or near-correct indexing terms is deemed useful even if these terms are not selected in the final indexing set. Their value lies in that they trigger the selection of a final indexing term. However, the downside of almost-correct recommendations is that they might confuse junior indexers who may not have sufficient training to distinguish between almost-correct and correct recommendations [7: 822–3].

A similar technique is applied in automated thesaurus construction. A computer program analyses words extracted from a text and the context they appear in. The program suggests these words as candidates for valid thesaurus descriptors with certain narrower or broader terms. The user can accept, reject or correct these suggestions.

A very popular method in experiments with automatic indexing is to compare the results of automatic indexing with the vocabulary of WordNet (*http://wordnet.princeton.edu*). Wordnet is a lexical database of the English language which not only gives synonyms but also related verbs, adjectives, etc. for each word. As it is permissable to download it, WordNet constitutes an ideal instrument for scientific research.

Automatic classification

Classification is not exactly the same as indexing; classification just puts documents in categories. But it has a good relation to indexing: normally the categories we use are based on the fact that the content of the documents is similar. Many experiments involving statistical methods have been conducted to find methods to automatically assign classification codes to texts.

Particularly for scientific papers, we could take into consideration the similarity in citation behaviour. The fundamental assumption here is that if two texts cite the same sources they must deal with the same subject(s). This is called bibliographic coupling. The same thing is true if the reference to two texts can be found in the bibliography of a third text (co-citation). Here, too, formulae to calculate the relative importance of these facts are in order; the simple fact that two references can be found together in more than one text is not enough to jump to conclusions. We will have to consider all the references in these texts. In principle the same techniques could be applied to hyperlinks in web documents.

Accepting all this, the next thing will be to choose a set of reference texts of which we know exactly what their subject is.

What can be expected of automatic text indexing?

Automatic text indexing has already been applied for many years in full-text databases, repositories, search engines, etc., but some of the applications are disappointing: simple word by word indexing, many errors, no advanced techniques, etc.

A lot of research is still going on. Since 1992 the place to be for advanced research in this field has been the TREC conferences. TREC is short for 'Text REtrieval Conference' where all world's specialists in automatic indexing share their results (see Figure 3.1). In order to make these results comparable, the tests are conducted on the same collections of texts. Although the papers presented at the TREC conferences are very technical, they show that a lot more is yet to come.

Figure 3.1 The main page of the TREC Conferences site (*http://trec.nist.gov/*)

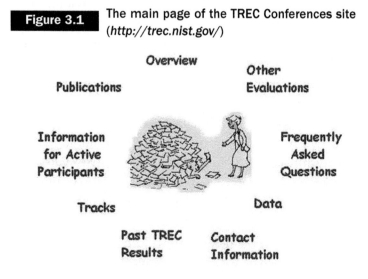

Overview

Other

Publications

Evaluations

Information for Active Participants

Frequently Asked Questions

Tracks

Data

Past TREC Results

Contact Information

TREC Economic Impact Study

TREC 2012 Call for Participation

TREC Statement on Product Testing and Advertising

The TREC Conference series is co-sponsored by the NIST Information Technology Laboratory's (ITL) Retrieval Group of the Information Access Division (IAD) Contact us at: trec (at) nist.gov

Figure 3.2 The Open Calais document viewer (*http://viewer. opencalais.com*)

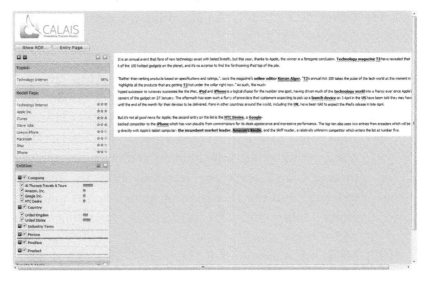

For those who do not believe in the power of automatic indexing, a glance at the Open Calais document viewer (*http://viewer.opencalais.com*) in Figure 3.2 can reveal something of its power. Just paste a text into the viewer and press the 'Submit' button. In a matter of seconds the whole text is indexed: all significant terms are extracted with their relative value, names of persons, cities, firms, rivers, historical facts, etc. are listed as such, and the whole text is classified to a general category.

References

[1] Moens, M.-F. (2000), *Automatic Indexing and Abstracting of Document Texts*. Boston: Kluwer Academic Publishers.

[2] See the LexisNexis user guide at *http://vlib.mmu.edu. my/2005/help/LexisNexisAcademicUserGuide.pdf*

[3] Porter, M.F. (1980), 'An algorithm for suffix stripping', *Program*, 14: 130–7.

[4] *http://www.googleguide.com/interpreting_queries.html*

[5] Braschler, M. and Ripplinger, B. (2004), 'How effective is stemming and decompounding for German text retrieval?', *Information Retrieval*, 7, 3–4: 291–316.

[6] Anderson, J.D. and Pérez-Carballo, J. (2001), 'The nature of indexing: how humans and machines analyze messages and texts for retrieval. Part II: machine indexing, and the allocation of human versus machine effort', *Information Processing and Management*, 37: 255–77.

[7] Névéol A, Shooshan S.E., Humphrey S.M., Mork J.G., Aronson A.R. *et al.* (2009), 'A recent advance in the automatic indexing of the biomedical literature', *Journal of Biomedical Informatics*, 42: 814–23.

4

Automatic indexing of images

Abstract: Basic techniques of automatic image indexing are discussed: context-based indexing, content-based indexing and automatic image annotation. Context-based indexing relies on the words surrounding the image and assumes that they express the content of the image. Content-based indexing uses one or more aspects of the image itself, e.g. the colour, the texture, etc. to make the image retrievable. Automatic image annotation compares some characteristics of the image to those of the images in a sample database which has been indexed manually. It assumes that images that have certain features in common express the same content. Although the engineering behind the three techniques may be quite advanced and difficult to understand, the essence of each one can be grasped by a few examples that are freely available on the web.

Key words: context-based image indexing, content-based image indexing, automatic image annotation, query by example.

Introduction

In an article on image indexing Joan Beaudoin writes: 'Visual materials offer a wealth of information that until recently was hidden due to limitations of physical access; the now nearly universal availability of images over the web underlines their importance. Hopefully, as their numbers continue to grow in the digital environment useful methods of image indexing can be discovered to ensure future access' [1]. In this chapter some of these new methods will be explained.

Images on the Internet

The Internet contains a vast quantity of pictures, drawings, photos and other kinds of graphical material. Many of them are not indexed at all; they were just put online by people who were looking for a way to save their photos or to share them with friends. Other images are integrated into web pages as illustrations, probably without any description of their content and even when they are accompanied by some kind of title or explanatory text, this is far from a controlled vocabulary term in a professional database, although controlled vocabularies to index graphical material, and especially works of art, have been constructed.

Two of them, the Art and Architecture Thesaurus (AAT) and the Thesaurus for Graphical Materials (TGM), have found users worldwide, mainly because of the prestige of the institutes they are connected to. The ATT, now containing more than 130 000 terms, has been developed from the late 1970s on and can be freely searched on the websites of the J. Paul Getty Trust [2]. It is a complex and highly professional thesaurus to index all kinds of graphical materials. The TGM of the Library of Congress Prints and Graphical Division was developed 'for subject indexing of pictorial materials, particularly the large general collections of historical images which are found in many libraries, historical societies, archives, and museums' [3]. In fact, it comes in two parts: TGM I and TGM II. TGM I contains about 6000 subject terms. TGM II, Genre and Physical Characteristic Terms, is about ten times smaller.

In her book on controlled vocabularies for art, architecture and other cultural works, Patricia Harpring gives an overview of vocabularies that can be used [4]. Besides the AAT and TGM she also discusses:

- The Getty Thesaurus of Geographical Names (TGN).
- The Union List of Artist Names (ULAN).
- The Cultural Objects Name Authority (CONA).
- The Conservation Thesaurus (CT).
- Chenhall's Nomenclature for Museum Cataloging.
- Iconclass.

Some of these instruments are authority name lists and one is a classification (Iconclass) and it could be subject to a whole discussion whether all of these instruments are 'vocabularies' or not, but at least the overview shows that there is no shortage of dedicated instruments to manually index works of art. With these instruments at hand it should be possible, in theory at least, to index a collection of photographs, posters or other graphical materials. And in fact this is done in the Getty, in the Library of Congress and in many other museums and libraries throughout the world. But is it still possible to do this for the large and rapidly growing collections of images on the Internet?

And there is more to worry about. In their book *Indexing Multimedia and Creative Works*, Pauline Rafferty and Rob Hidderley are pessimistic about the possibility of indexing multimedia adequately by controlled vocabulary because one single work can have as many interpretations as it has users [5]. As in many other books or articles on the interpretation of art, the authors refer to the renowned theories of the art historian Erwin Panofsky (1892–1968), who made a distinction between three different levels of meaning in an art work:

- the primary or natural subject matter: e.g. what a painting represents, e.g. a woman holding a little child;
- the secondary or conventional subject matter: e.g. we understand that this woman is the Blessed Mary holding Christ;
- the intrinsic meaning or content: e.g. the interpretation of this work in its historical context, the aesthetic value of the work, etc.

The challenge in indexing art consists of grasping all three levels, and the point Rafferty and Hidderley want to make is that it not possible to do so. They also doubt whether there could be one single system to store and retrieve multimedia. But who needs this? First of all a distinction has to be made between indexing and information retrieval: indexing is mostly a preliminary action to information retrieval. Although the title of their book says that it is about 'indexing', the authors are dealing with 'information retrieval' most of the time. The result of indexing is a set of data (index terms) which can be searched for. The retrieval normally will use this data, but it is highly depending on its own characteristics: the interface, the possibility to use Boolean operators (AND, OR, NOT), specialized techniques like truncation, stemming and the like. Both retrieval and indexing have their own problems and instruments.

Without indexing no data can be found, at least in most cases, but it is not entirely impossible to retrieve non-indexed data: in texts one can find a particular word or word combination by searching sequentially, i.e. by comparing each string of characters to the search term. Secondly, multimedia are very diverse; it is not necessary to have one single system to retrieve all kinds; there might be all sorts of information retrieval systems, based on different indexing techniques, serving different needs.[1]

Not all images we can find on the Internet or in image collections are meant to be works of art, but every image has the potential to arouse many different interpretations. A simple and hastily taken photograph by a journalist of Che Guevara looking out over the crowds at a meeting has meant so much in the lives of all the people that it is one of the most meaningful images of the second half of the twentieth century. All the youngsters who hang this picture on the walls of their bedrooms or wear T-shirts on which it was printed could tell their own story about it. Does this mean that we should forget about indexing images – and certainly about letting machines do this for us, or that we should share the frustrations of Rafferty and Hidderly? There still is a need to get a grip on the vast amount of graphical material we are confronted with, especially on the Internet. People want to find pictures and see things, and some of the new automatic indexing techniques can help, although some of them are still very much experimental.

In this chapter we will explain the essence of three kinds of automatic indexing for graphical materials: context-based indexing, content-based indexing and automatic image annotation. The first one is based on texts found next to the images, the second one on characteristics of the image itself. The third one automatically adds index terms to images based on examples. We will meet variations of these principles in the indexing of other multimedia works: moving images (films, videos) and music. Another alternative to manual indexing by use of controlled vocabularies is the highly popular form of manual indexing of images by tagging, which is the subject of Chapter 9.

Some confusion might exist between context- and text-based indexing; sometimes these two concepts are used as synonyms, sometimes they mean different things. We can call text-based indexing all kinds of indexing that makes use of words, i.e.

- indexing by means of manual added controlled vocabulary terms;
- tagging;
- context-based indexing.

Context-based indexing

Context-based indexing makes little or no use of the graphical elements of the picture. It looks at the context in which the picture is placed and filters out text elements surrounding it, in the hope that these provide an adequate description of what is represented in the illustration. Although systems that use context-based indexing are not likely to reveal their secrets, it is not very difficult to grasp their basic assumptions:

- a caption under an image is a good indicator of the image's content;
- an alternate text for the image in the HTML code is undoubtedly a very good translation of what is in the image;
- any word near to the image is probably telling more about it than words that are further remote in the text;
- nouns or names of persons, cities, etc. may be good candidates as keywords to the image.

These, and maybe some other parameters, have to be mixed into an algorithm which will take into account the relative weight of every element.

A very good example of the results of this technique is the Google images database (*http://images.google.com*). Google screens web pages and stores the images on it into its database, assuming that accompanying text elements indeed have a lot to do with the subject of the image. In the FAQ pages Google states that it takes its indexing terms from many parts of the text pages out of which the images were taken: 'Google analyzes the text on the page adjacent to the image, the image caption and dozens of other factors to determine the image content.'

Of course, Google is very vague about the 'dozens of other factors', as this is one of its many corporate secrets. Everything goes well as long as those text elements are meant to describe the true content of the image, but if I were to make a web page of myself and wrote the text 'This is not Albert Einstein' under it, I would probably end in the Google image database as 'Albert Einstein'.

A search for a simple subject is usually successful and gives only a small amount of noise, e.g.

- 'elephants' results in pictures or drawings of elephants, but also in an image of a map and one of a teapot;
- 'money' will produce images of bank notes, but also the photo of people called John Money or Bob Money;
- 'cars' leads to images of all sorts of cars, but also to screen prints of databases or computer programmes about cars.

Even more complex searches have good results, although more unsuitable images will come up, e.g.

- two men on bikes
- cat eating a mouse
- ship leaving the harbour
- small yellow car
- dog wearing hat
- children eating apples

The advantages and disadvantages can easily be seen in searches for a certain person by his or her name: if you know this person, you will recognize his or her photo. But if you do not know the person by sight you will not be sure which of the photographs Google presents you is of that person. Google will connect all the names on a webpage to the images it contains. Consequently, if the page lists the names of many people and their photographs, the system is doomed to mingle them.

Another of the downsides of content-based indexing is that images which are merely accompanied by some meaningless number generated by a digital camera or by a computer programme can only be found if one knows that number. Any kind of number, e.g. '02.jpg' or '789564' will retrieve many photos, mostly from digital photo albums.

Two web applications built by Grant Robinson from New Zealand illustrate the accuracy of the concept-oriented indexing by Google's image database. The first, called 'Montage-a-Google' (*http://grant.robinson.name/projects/montage-a-google/*), asks the user to enter a search term by which it will retrieve 20 images from the Google database in order to form a large collage (see Figure 4.1). The purpose of the application is to make pictures for desktops or posters. Entering a term like 'house' will of course retrieve a majority of pictures of houses, but also some of dog houses, landscapes or even aeroplanes.

The second application by Grant Robinson, 'Guess the Google', is a web game: *http://grant.robinson.name/projects/guess-the-google*. Twenty images from Google are presented to the player, who has 20 seconds to guess their keyword in Google's images database (Figure 4.2). Some are obvious and easy to guess, others just impossible.

From 2007 until 2011 Google placed a game on its image site, the 'Google Image Labeler' (now defunct). Playing this

Figure 4.1 'Montage-a-Google' (*http://grant.robinson.name/ projects/montage-a-google/*)

Figure 4.2 'Guess the Google' (*http://grant.robinson.name/ projects/guess-the-google*)

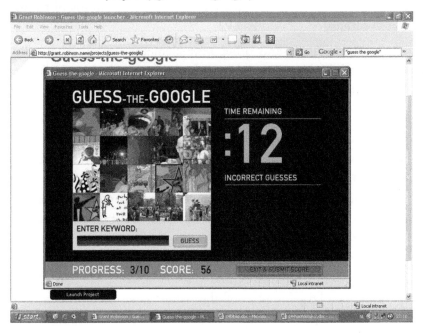

game, everybody could help Google label its images. Two 'labelers' assigned keywords to the same images the system presented and got points when their keywords matched. Google explicitly presented this feature as a tool to 'help improve the quality of Google's image search results', i.e. to overcome the limits of its first images indexing tool, context-oriented indexing. Games like this one are a new phenomenon on the web: as they are not created for fun alone but to realise a certain goal for the creators they are called 'games with a purpose'. Google's index is based on natural language, but it is possible to link index terms which are extracted from the text to controlled vocabularies, e.g. the AAT, the TGM or others.

Text elements for indexing can also be extracted from the image itself, using optical character recognition (OCR). This technique has found applications in the world of law and order and espionage, e.g.

- licence plate numbers are extracted from photos of traffic offences;
- street names and other text elements are automatically read in large quantities of photos made by planes or satellites.

In libraries and archives this technique could render services when large amounts of photos are digitalized and indexed. They could also be useful to index photo collections on the Internet. Indeed, some of those photos contain text elements that tell something about their content, e.g. dates, texts on shop windows, road signs, names of places or events printed on old postcards, etc.

Jung *et al.* [6] give an overview of research on text extraction from images (and video) and conclude that: 'Even though a large number of algorithms have been proposed in the literature, no single method can provide satisfactory performance in all the applications due to the large variations in character font, size, texture, color, etc.' [6: 993]. This does not mean that it is not possible to get good results; we only need to develop different tools according to the nature of the material we want to index. Although we could still call these techniques 'text-based', they no longer take index terms from texts that surround the image; the text is part of the image itself.

Content-based indexing

In content-based indexing not only text elements, but all sorts of characteristics of the image are used to guess what it is about: colour, shapes, texture, background, geometrical forms, etc. These techniques, too, proved to be useful in security and policing, e.g. they enable identification of wanted persons in photographs of crowds, and the medical world also applies these techniques to analyse imaging material.

Even text-based image search engines like Google's Image Search can easily integrate some content-based elements. In Google's Advanced Image Search the user can choose between 'black and white', 'any color' and 'full color', which are characteristics of the image itself. Of course, this is relatively easy because every colour has its digital code. More difficult would be to automatically select images that contain circular or rectangular shapes from a collection and far more difficult is to retrieve images of lions, small cars, a tree, a butterfly, etc.

A lot of specialized research is still going on, and most of the results are used to build commercial software. But some applications on the web give a good impression of what these techniques can do in information retrieval. However, the drawback is that many of these sites are the result of research projects and cease to exist after the end of the project. A typical example was Webseek. This was an interesting content-based search engine from Columbia University (located at *http://persia.ee.columbia.edu:8008*). The user started by browsing through the subject categories and selected one image as an example for the others he or she wanted to find in the Webseek database or on the web. The search engine basically searched for the same colour scheme, which retrieved lots of noise, i.e. pictures with the same colours but totally different content. In Figure 4.3, the first photo of the jeep was used to find similar images. None of them contain a jeep, or even a car, although the colour schemes match the example.

A second example of this 'query by example' – or better still: 'query by visual example' technique can be found at *http://labs.systemone.at/retrievr*, a web application by

Figure 4.3   A content-based search at Webseek

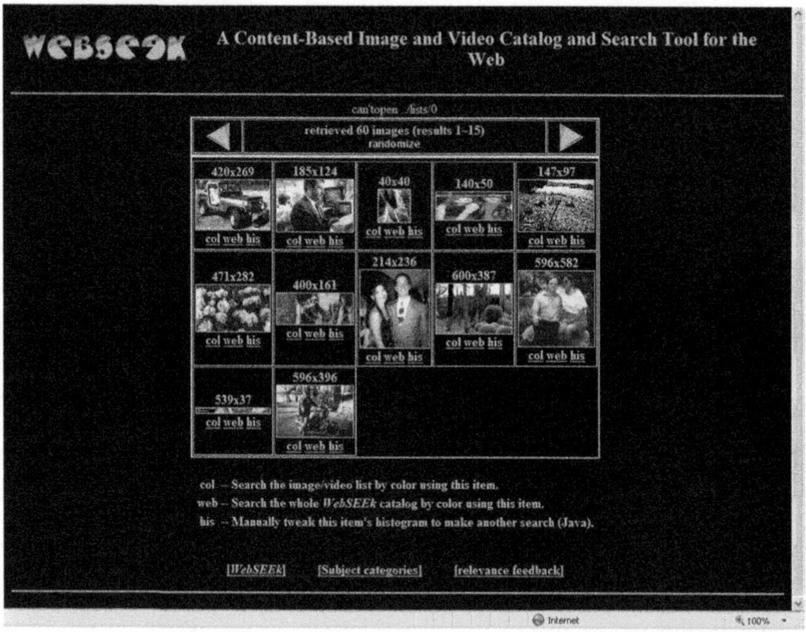

Christian Langreiter. The user chooses a colour from the colour pallet and draws a picture with the cursor and instantaneously the system retrieves a set of images from the Flickr database that match the drawing, as in Figure 4.4. The results are sometimes astonishingly good, even with a rather rudimentary example. As an alternative, try it with your own image.

Langreiter based his website on the work of three researchers from the University of Washington back in 1995: Chuck Jacobs, Adam Finkelstein and David Salesin [7]. They used a mathematical technique called the wavelet transformation to index images in an image database and did

Figure 4.4 Query by example: the images on the right-hand side of the screen should match the example drawn in the search box on the left-hand side

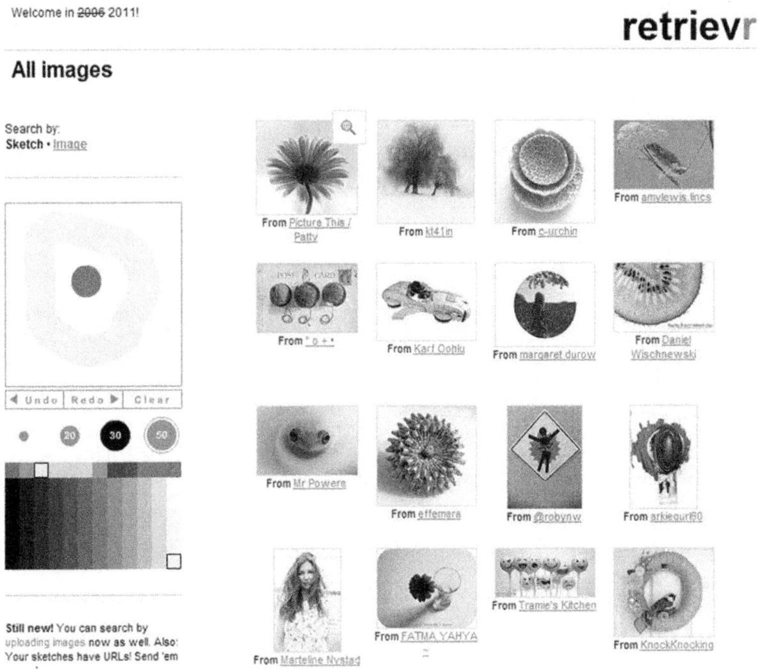

Welcome in ~~2006~~ 2011!

retrievr

All images

Search by:
Sketch · Image

◀ Undo | Redo ▶ | Clear

● | 20 | 30 | 50

Still new! You can search by uploading images now as well. Also: Your sketches have URLs! Send 'em

From Picture This / Patty
From kt41n
From c-urchin
From amviewis.lincs

From °o+°
From Karl Oohki
From margaret durow
From Daniel Wischnewski

From Mr Powers
From effemera
From @robynw
From arkiegurl60

From Marteline Nystad
From FATMA YAHYA
From Tramie's Kitchen
From KnockKnocking

the same with the example image. The result of the latter is matched against the index of the image database and the corresponding images are retrieved. Although the mathematics behind this may be complicated, the principles are simple and show clearly the difference between context-based and content-based indexing. A – rather archaic – drawing in their paper illustrates it all, as can be seen in Figure 4.5.

One of the commercial applications of content-based image indexing, the QBIC-system, was made by IBM and used to index the collection of the State Hermitage Museum

Figure 4.5 The drawing by Jacob, Finkelstein and Salesin explaining the technique behind content-based indexing and retrieval [7]

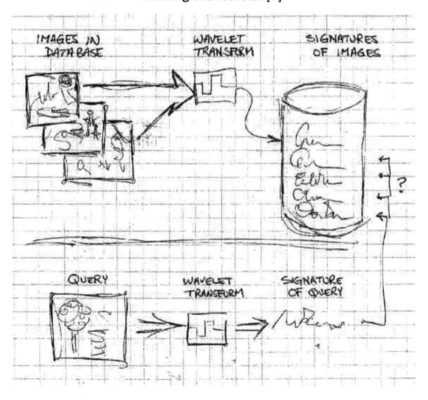

in St Petersburg (*http://www.hermitagemuseum.org/fcgi-bin/db2www/qbicSearch.mac/qbic?selLang=English*). QBIC stands for 'query by image content', and although it is still called 'experimental' the technique has been implemented on the Hermitage website for some years now. The programme presents two types of search to the user: the colour search, as in Figure 4.6, and the layout search seen in Figure 4.7. In the colour search the user composes a colour palette which will be matched against the paintings in the Hermitage Museum. A green bottom half and a blue upper half will most likely represent paintings of landscapes, whereas a light blue bottom half may find paintings of a sea – although many unpredictable results might pop up.

Figure 4.6 Searching by colour palette at the State Hermitage Museum in St Petersburg

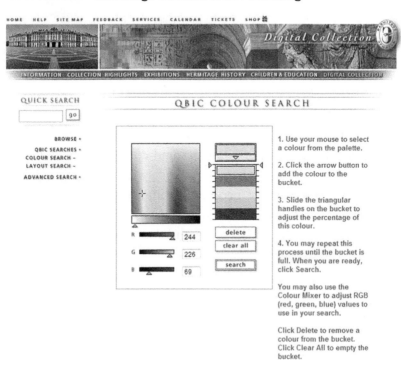

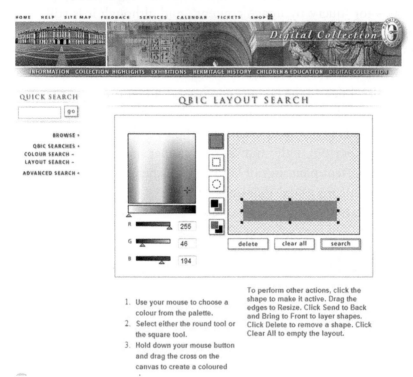

Figure 4.7 Searching by layout at the State Hermitage Museum in St Petersburg

The layout search offers more possibilities: the user can make a composition of shapes and colours. A yellow circle on top and a black square underneath will most likely retrieve portraits of people wearing black cloths, a red or yellow circle and a blue square may be a sunset above the ocean, etc. The success of the retrieval depends on the inspiration of the user, but some paintings seem to pop up over and over again.

In September 2011 Google added some content-based features to its images search engine. Now it is possible to search for a specific colour whereas Google only used to offer the choice between black and white, gray scale or colour. It is now also possible to ask for similar images. As in the example in Figure 4.8, if you start from a search for 'flowers' you will get images of flowers in different colours. Suppose you now click on a picture of a yellow flower; you will get it in a pop-up window. Now you can click on 'Similar' which will retrieve you more images of yellow flowers. It is also possible to sort the images by subject. As usual, Google does not give away the secrets behind its new features, but it will bring content-based indexing to the attention of a large public.

Content-based image retrieval (CBIR) is indeed promising, and the fact that Google integrates it in its search engine proves this, but it may not be as powerful yet as (con)text-based image retrieval, because words may still be a better instrument to build complex search terms, or, as Tsai *et al.* note: 'Current CBIR systems index and retrieve images based on their low-level features, such as colour, texture, and shape, and it is difficult to find desired images based on these low-level features, because they have no direct correspondence to high-level concepts in humans' minds. This is the so-called semantic gap problem' [8].

Figure 4.8 Content-based features in Google image search

Automatic image annotation

Although some of the more advanced examples of content-based indexing and 'query by visual example' (QBVE) are rather spectacular, QBVE has a few disadvantages. The indexing is semantically poor. Only basic characteristics of an image are indexed: colours, textures, shapes, etc. There is no way to indicate what makes an image sad or cheerful; there is also no way to tell that an image contains young children or middle-aged people, etc., let alone that we could trace more complex or abstract subjects. On the other hand, the retrieval depends on the user's ability to find or draw suitable examples in order to launch these at the database in a query.

Automatic image annotation tries to overcome these disadvantages and still offer the possibility to index large collections of images automatically. The principle is rather simple. At first a set of images is indexed manually using free-text annotations, keywords, terms from a controlled vocabulary, an ontology or from a classification. These images will serve as models in the indexing process. All images in the database will be compared automatically with these models. Every image that shows the same characteristics as one of the models will get the same index terms. All depends on the quality of the model database, the vocabulary and the way the images are analysed and processed. The process involves algorithms to extract the relevant features in every image, and artificial intelligence to train the system how to compare these successfully with the models. It goes without saying that this is still subject to advanced research.[2]

Notwithstanding the simplicity of the principle, it still may be a problem to index a substantial model collection. Many techniques have been tested to find an economical way to index the model collection:

- the use of a tagged image collection like Flickr;
- the use of 'games with a purpose' in which the aid of enthusiastic volunteers is demanded;
- conversion of an existing already-indexed collection;
- etc.

The result may have several advantages:

- The user no longer uses QBVE, but 'query by semantic example' (QBSE): he or she just uses words and can search for complex subjects. Also synonyms, homonyms and all complex relations between terms can now be treated the same way they are in a manual system based on a controlled vocabulary.
- The indexing goes way beyond simple concepts. Whereas content based indexing only results in classifying images according to rather meaningless characteristics, now the indexing process may label images as expressing a very complex subject.

Mixed techniques

Recently, mixed methods are being developed. Deniz Kılınç and Adil Alpkocak report on their research into a method to combine the context-based and automatic image annotation method, which they call 'annotation-based image retrieval' [9]. They choose material from Wikipedia, which is ideal for a content-based index, because the images clearly correlate highly with the content of the text in which they appear; they are never meaningless illustrations. They analyse the texts surrounding the image and process it using well-known text processing techniques like the removal of stop words. After that the words from these texts are expanded by adding supplementary terms (synonyms, etc.) from the WordNet dictionary (*http://wordnetweb.princeton.edu/perl/webwn*). WordNet is very popular as a base for creating controlled vocabularies and automatic indexing tools. The results now are used to create new searches on the material. After this, ranking algorithms are used to present the results to the user.

From the content-based indexing these researchers assume that the text in which the image is embedded tells something about its subject. On the other hand they try to overcome the disadvantages of content-based indexing by searching for a method to automatically stick more suitable keywords onto the images. This research is still in an experimental stage and at this moment it is not clear whether this method will generate acceptable results for other material than Wikipedia images.

The purpose of it all

All these researches and experiments are fascinating, but what practical use can they have? First of all they try to get a grip on the vast amount of images on the Internet. As images are a source of information, people want to retrieve them in order to look at them. That explains the success of Google images or Flickr.

In professions where the information extracted from images is very important and where many images have to be processed each day, these techniques could facilitate the workload involved and thus save money. A good example here is the automatic processing of medical images. Also, in the work of security and policing, many images have to be analysed daily. As I am writing this, an important city close by my town announced that it is going to install cameras covering all incoming traffic. From each car, the licence plate will be read automatically and when a stolen car or a car belonging to an individual who is wanted by the police is detected, an alarm will go off in a police station. Big Brother clearly knows the advantages of context-based image retrieval.

Notes

1. Rafferty and Hidderly find a solution for their philosophical constrains in what they call 'democratic indexing', an indexing technique we will discuss elsewhere in this book under the name of 'folksonomy'.
2. An overview of the techniques can be found in Zhang, D., Monirul I.M. and Lu, G. (2011), 'A review on automatic image annotation techniques', *Pattern Recognition*, 10.1016/j. patcog.2011.05.013; or in Hanbury, A. (2008), 'A survey of methods for image annotation', *Journal of Visual Languages & Computing*, 19: 617–27.

References

[1] Beaudoin, J. (2006), 'Interindexer consistency: term usage, and indexer experience levels in the application of image descriptors', *Proceedings of the America Society for Information Science and Technology*, 43: 1–7.
[2] *http://www.getty.edu/research/conducting_research/ vocabularies/aat*
[3] *http://www.loc.gov/rr/print/tgm1/ia.html*
[4] Harpring, P. (2010), *Introduction to Controlled Vocabularies: Terminology for Art, Architecture, and other Cultural Works*. Los Angeles: Getty Research Institute.

[5] Rafferty, P. and Hidderley, R. (2005), *Indexing Multimedia and Creative Works: the Problem of Meaning and Interpretation*. Farnham, Surrey: Ashgate.

[6] Jung, K., Kim, K.I. and Jain, A.K. (2004), 'Text information extraction in images and video: a survey', *Pattern recognition*, 37: 977–97.

[7] Jacobs, C., Finkelstein, A. and Salesin, D. (1995), 'Fast multiresolution image querying', Research paper. Available from: *http://grail.cs.washington.edu/projects/query/*

[8] Tsai, C-.F., McGarry, K. and Tait, J. (2006), 'Qualitative evaluation of automatic assignment of keywords to images', *Information Processing and Management*, 42: 137.

[9] Kilinç, D. and Alpkocak, A. (2011), 'An expansion and reranking approach for annotation-based image retrieval from Web', *Expert Systems with Applications*, 38: 1312–27.

5

The black art of indexing moving images

Abstract: Moving images are still indexed manually, but the overwhelming amount of video fragments makes it necessary to look for automatic indexing techniques. Because many videos contain spoken texts, text recognition can be applied to extract text, which then can be indexed using methods designed for automatic text indexing. Keyframe indexing extracts the most meaningful images from video fragments. It can be compared with the automatic generation of a table of contents of a written text.

Key words: automatic video indexing, keyframe indexing.

Manual indexing of moving images

Librarians have experience with indexing films, videos and DVDs: they simply use the same methods they have for indexing books: non-fiction DVDs and videos are provided with thesaurus terms or codes taken from the main classification, fiction is indexed with genre terms, etc. Libraries that offer DVDs for loan describe them in their catalogues, using the same MAchine-Readable Cataloging (MARC) format they use for books. These instruments have proven their worth for more than a century in libraries and they have been applied for collections of videos since the

1970s. However, there is one condition: the material must be complete, i.e. have a finished nature.

Fragmentary material, on the other hand, is dealt with in archives, audiovisual archives as well as paper ones. But while only few people are interested in fragments of written information, there is a big market for video fragments, and of course this can now be found on the Internet. Commercial firms which sell film clips index them by adding a lot of keywords, in order to let the customer find what he needs in as many ways as possible. A 25-second clip for sale of pigs in a Bavarian Alpine field at GettyImages[1] gets these keywords: 'Tranquil Scene', 'Nature', 'Outdoors', 'Rural Scene', 'Grazing', 'Bavaria', 'Cloud', 'Evergreen Tree', 'Hill', 'Mountain Peak', 'Day', 'Lake', 'Color Image', 'Domestic pig', 'Grass', 'Bavarian Alps', 'Real time', 'Cinematography', 'Zoom in', 'Medium group of animals', 'Nobody', 'Livestock', '20 seconds or greater', '2006'. Anybody who enters one of these keywords, e.g. 'Nobody' or 'Day', can retrieve (and buy) the clip of the group of pigs – and this is of course the purpose.

Major television stations archive their material with an added description of it, e.g.

- President George Bush Jr. playing with a dog in front of the White House, 135 frames.
- Panoramic shot of students in exam room, 123 frames.

Manual video indexing has the same advantages as manual text indexing:

- Normally it is well done.
- One can make use of instruments that have proved to be reliable: controlled vocabularies, classifications, etc.

A commercial firm or a library with a limited collection can find the resources to add a controlled vocabulary term or many keywords to each video, DVD or clip. But what about indexing all the millions of clips on e.g. YouTube? Confronted with this vast amount of video material any traditional method would be too expensive, too slow and not detailed enough. Of course, one can ask everybody who uploads a clip to add some keywords or else ask all viewers to submit comments – and this is exactly how it is done on video sites. In Chapter 9 we will look into this practice in more detail, but maybe we would also like techniques to process large video archives without having to rely on the unpredictable reactions of the anonymous public.

Why index moving images automatically?

So, is there any reason why one should want to index moving images automatically? Yes, there are a few:

- Manual indexing is slow and expensive, unless we ask a lot of people to do it, for free, like on YouTube and other clip sites.

- But then it is unpredictable and it could be superficial.

- The material to index can be overwhelming: a TV news station probably gets dozens of videos about sport events in one weekend. It may be interesting to have a technique that automatically reduces a one and a half hour video of a football match into one of only a few minutes containing all the interesting scenes, e.g. the goals.

- We may want more in-depth indexing. Where in a 30-minute interview does the president mention oil prices? And where does he say anything about his concern about preschool education? It is not enough to have keywords like 'President' and 'Interview' to find this. We can only do this kind of indexing manually if we have unlimited resources – which normally are not available.

Good techniques for automatic indexing may solve all of this. Basically there are three sorts of techniques:

Indexing based on speech or text recognition

Since the release of *The Jazz Singer* in 1927 most films have been spoken. It is possible to transcribe the sound track of a film or documentary with speech recognition software. After that, automatic text indexing can be applied. Nowadays this is done with videotaped interviews, conferences and news fragments.

The American Public Broadcasting Service uses speech recognition to index news clips from television stations. Every word or sequence of words can be searched at *http://www.pbs.org/newshour/video*, as can be seen in Figure 5.1. Of course you will find many answers to searches for 'Iraq' or 'global warming', but it is interesting to test this technique with less meaningful words or word combinations like:

Damned

Haircut

Fitness

Bikes

For each fragment you can click the 'Read the transcript' button on the site and see a full transcript of the dialogues. A few years ago, the site gave a better insight into the techniques behind indexing by speech recognition. Selecting a term from the drop down box next to a clip brought you directly to the fragment where that particular word of group of words was

Figure 5.1 **Example of index terms on the American Public Broadcasting Service website**

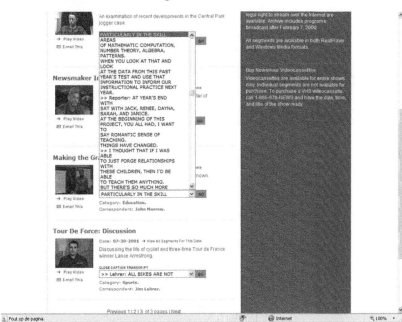

pronounced. Some of the index terms make sense, others were quite nonsensical, e.g.

- but never makes any
- very
- talking to this week have
- process, and called for
- and for a newspaper to
- and I think it was felt that

Another example of the same technique can be found at *http://www.tveyes.com*. By clicking on an image one can go directly to the fragment where the search term was spoken, as in Figure 5.2.

Figure 5.2 Searching for 'inflation' at TVeyes.com

Speech recognition is of little use when we do not understand the language. In that case capturing and indexing the subtitles with translations can be a solution. This process is not as straightforward as transforming text printed on a paper sheet into digitalized text. Since the 1980s optical character recognition (OCR) of printed – or even of handwritten – text has advanced enormously. OCR software was very expensive and not all that accurate; conversely, good applications are downloadable for free on the Internet today. Excellent software usually comes bundled with scanners or printer-scanners, even with cheap ones.

The difficult part in indexing subtitles is not OCR, but what comes before that, i.e. text information extraction (TIE). The software has to locate and filter out those parts of the images that contain the text – and 'moving pictures' are in that respect no different from still images. After this it has to process the text zones in order to get the text good enough to serve as input of the OCR software.[2] The final stage of the process is indexing the text file, which is, of course, pretty much the same as indexing text captured by speech recognition.

On the Internet one can download subtitles in many languages to almost all popular films and also software to synchronize these subtitles with the films. This has nothing to do with indexing, but all the more with – illegally or legally – downloading of films.

There is no shortage of methods in this field and ingenious techniques are developed and reported – the only problem they leave is that we cannot see much of the results yet. To give an idea of what is going on, let us look at what two researchers report on their tests with Turkish news videos [1]. They first divide the raw video files into individual news stories, based upon the silences in the audio material. Each fragment is fed into an automatic text extractor, which tries to extract the spoken tests and sends this to a speech recognizer. The result is a written text, which can be analysed using different methods. The first one is called 'named entry recognition', meaning that each word or word combination is matched against a database with names of people, places, etc. Also words like 'today' or 'yesterday' are interpreted according to the actual date of the news broadcast.

A second technique, the 'person entity extraction and coreference resolution' tries to correlate the names of persons to their professions or organizations. The 'automatic hyperlinking' links the information that is found in the clip to the content of news articles on the web in order to enrich the information. The 'semantic event extraction' procedure tries to find suitable keywords for each event in the news broadcast using statistical methods. Also, the production metadata (e.g. the broadcast date) is taken as a source of additional information. Although the whole procedure is mainly based on speech recognition, it is enriched with references to databases, texts on the web and other external information, which makes it similar to automatic image annotation techniques.

Keyframe indexing

An index extracts the most meaningful words from a written text and presents them in an alphabetical list. Keyframe indexing applies the same kind of technique to moving images: it extracts those images which are considered to have a high information value and presents them in an overview. Someone who wants to check if the content of a book is interesting may browse the index before spending the time on reading it. In the same way someone who wants to evaluate a video clip can browse the keyframes. A good example of this can be found at the Open Video Project (*http://www.open-video.org*). In one glance the user can evaluate the content of the clip before downloading it, as in Figure 5.3. This could be compared with having a look at the table of content or at the index of a book. Mostly one can also play the video clip in fast forward, which again could be compared to reading the summary of a book or an article.

A clip has to go through more than one stage before this result can be reached. In general a video fragment consists of:

- frames, i.e. different images;
- shots, i.e. the many frames that follow each other and build one unity;
- cuts, i.e. the places where one shot ends and another begins;
- scenes, i.e. more than one shot, together forming a unity.

Figure 5.3 Keyframe indexing at open-video.org

Shot boundary detection (SBD) is the technique to isolate the different shots in a video clip. This is still the subject of a lot of specialized research trying to develop better methods of SBD. One of these techniques consists of comparing the colour combinations of the frames; as long as the difference between two consecutive frames is not too big one could suppose they are parts of the same scene. When the difference reaches a certain limit a new shot must be beginning. In the TV news shots are embedded between two 'anchor shots', i.e. relatively stable shots with one person sitting in the studio and talking. It is also possible to determine the nature of a shot, e.g.

- A speech would consist of the upper part of a person of which mainly the mouth moves.

- A meeting is a room with many people looking straight ahead.

- In a shot of a person walking or running the figure moves up and down.

But there are many pitfalls, e.g.

- A face can be partly covered by clothing or hair.
- A shot of a meeting can be taken from the back of the room showing only the back view of the people present.

When the shots are separated from each other, the most representative frames from each shot can be selected: these are the keyframes. More than one technique could be used to select a keyframe:

- The frame that matches the average values in colour, etc. of the shot.
- The first frame.
- The last frame.
- The middle frame.

Smeaton remarks that this 'is regarded as a "black art"' [2: 385].

The future of video indexing

There is more to come in video indexing. Some of the factors pushing this are:

- The enormous numbers of clips on video sites that need to be indexed automatically.
- Commercial firms that sell video fragments will pay for the development of indexing techniques in order to get a grip on the mass of clips they want to index.
- The need to process surveillance videos automatically. More and more cameras are placed in public places. This confronts authorities with the dilemma whether they

should pay personnel to watch all these recordings or invest in automatic processing of it.

In 2001 the Text REtrieval Conference (TREC) sponsored 'a video "track" devoted to research in automatic segmentation, indexing, and content-based retrieval of digital video' [3]. In 2003 this 'track' became an independent organization, TRECVID, which organizes annual conferences on video indexing. TRECVID uses the same strategy as TREC: experts test new methods and techniques on a set of video clips. The annual conferences are an international forum for experts to exchange information and research results.

The main topics in the most recent TRECVID conferences are:

- Know-item search task: how to find a video fragment one knows?
- Semantic indexing: automatic assignment of keywords to fragments.
- Content-based multimedia copy detection: how can we find out if a fragment is a copy made from another video? This is especially important for copyright reasons.
- Event detection in airport surveillance videos: how can suspicious behaviour be detected automatically in surveillance videos?
- Multimedia event detection: which video covers a certain event?
- Instance search: how can we automatically detect a certain person, place, object in videos?

Because every researcher is expected to work on a predefined set of videos the results are highly comparable and the better method can be detected easily.

Notes

1. GettyImages can be found at: *http://editorial.gettyimages.com/ Footage/FootageHome.aspx*
2. An overview of different techniques can be found in Jung, K., Kim, K.I. and Jain, A.K. (2004), 'Text information extraction in image and video: a survey', *Pattern Recognition*, 37: 977–97.

References

[1] Küçuk, D. and Yazici A. (2011), 'Exploiting information extration techniques for automatic semantic video indexing with an application to Turkish news videos', *Knowledge-based Systems*, 24: 844–57.

[2] Smeaton, Alan F. (2004), 'Indexing, browsing and searching of digital video', *Annual Review of Information Science and Technology*, 38: 371–407.

[3] *http://www-nlpir.nist.gov/projects/trecvid/*

6

Automatic indexing of music

Abstract: Traditional music indexing treats music recordings mainly in the same way as text documents: it tries to express content in subject headings. The Internet made it possible to search for music fragments by entering the music itself as a 'question'. In order to retrieve the music fragments that match this 'question' from a database certain mathematical techniques must be applied, which are already implemented in some (experimental) music retrieval sites.

Key words: automatic music indexing, query by humming, query by representation.

Introduction

Traditionally, songs and other musical works are indexed by textual elements: the title, the name of the composer, the name of the orchestra or the singer(s), terms from specialized thesauri, etc. In public libraries, music CDs are catalogued according to the same rules as books. They are treated as objects that can be loaned by the public and their description is provided with a shelf number based on a classification and a subject heading from a controlled vocabulary list. In her book on the Library of Congress Subject Headings, Vanda Broughton writes: 'There are no widely used specialist controlled vocabularies for music, and, apart from its use in general libraries, LCSH is probably the most substantial subject cataloguing tool available to music librarians' [1].

This was already so before the existence of music databases or the Internet, in the ages of paper card library catalogues and printed music encyclopaedias, and it is very surprising that it still is the case. Audiovisual librarians felt that subject headings designed to index books are not sufficient when they wanted to index music recordings. They normally have some additional instruments, e.g. lists of music genres or a music classification. And still they may not be satisfied. The Flemish public libraries use global indexing for their book collection: books get one or a few subject headings, while in-depth indexing is applied to music CDs: each track is catalogued and gets subject headings, genres, etc.

But all that is of little help if you wake up with part of a song going on and on in your head and you wonder what this song could be. You can simply type in those words in one of many popular (and mostly commercial) 'find that song' sites on the Internet. The answer will be the title of songs that contain that particular sequence of words. Asking for 'you can never leave' instantly gives nine titles on *http://www.endlesslyrics.com*, among which is *Hotel California* by the Eagles. The speed with which the answer pops up is amazing. In the 1980s you probably had to call a local radio station to find a DJ who might know a lot of song texts by heart in order to find out the title of the song.

The indexing techniques behind this kind of search engine are very good and the retrieval is fast, but they are useless if you only remember a certain melody – or part of it. Wouldn't it be nice to be able to find which song corresponds to a tune you just vaguely remember? Well, it is possible.

Some examples of music retrieval

In general there are two methods for music retrieval:

- *Query by humming/singing/whistling/tapping.* This can be compared to query by example in text databases: the searcher hums or sings part of the song or he taps the rhythm on the space bar of his computer. The system then will give all fragments or all songs that correspond to this melody or rhythm.

- *Query by representation.* The searcher uses some kind of graphical representation of the melody of the song he wants to find. In music this could of course be music notes, but it might just as well be some other form of graphical representation of notes: characters or other symbols.

Let's look at some examples of retrieval sites. Here, only a few freely available sites are discussed.

Musipedia

Musipedia (*http://www.musipedia.org/*) offers different ways to search for music by using non-textual methods (see Figure 6.1):

- 'Keyboard search': the searcher must try to play the tone by clicking on the keyboard in the site (a nicer interface is provide under the option 'Flash Piano').

- 'Contour search': the searcher must try to enter the 'Parsons Code' of the song, i.e. the sequence of notes going up or down in the pitch.

- 'By microphone': here the searcher can sing or hum or whistle the melody.

- 'Rhythm search': here you can tap the rhythm on the space bar of the computer.

Figure 6.1 Musipedia

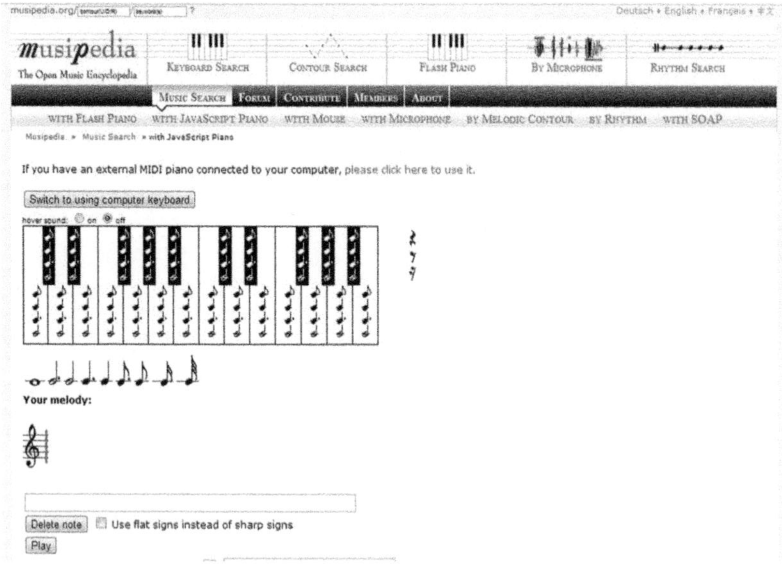

Themefinder

In the Themefinder (*http://www.themefinder.com/*) search form (see Figure 6.2) you can enter different characteristics of a piece of music: the pitch, the interval, etc. These must be represented in numbers or characters as it is not easy to type music notes on a normal PC keyboard – although the way Themefinder wants you to symbolise music characteristics is not that easy either.

Figure 6.2 Themefinder

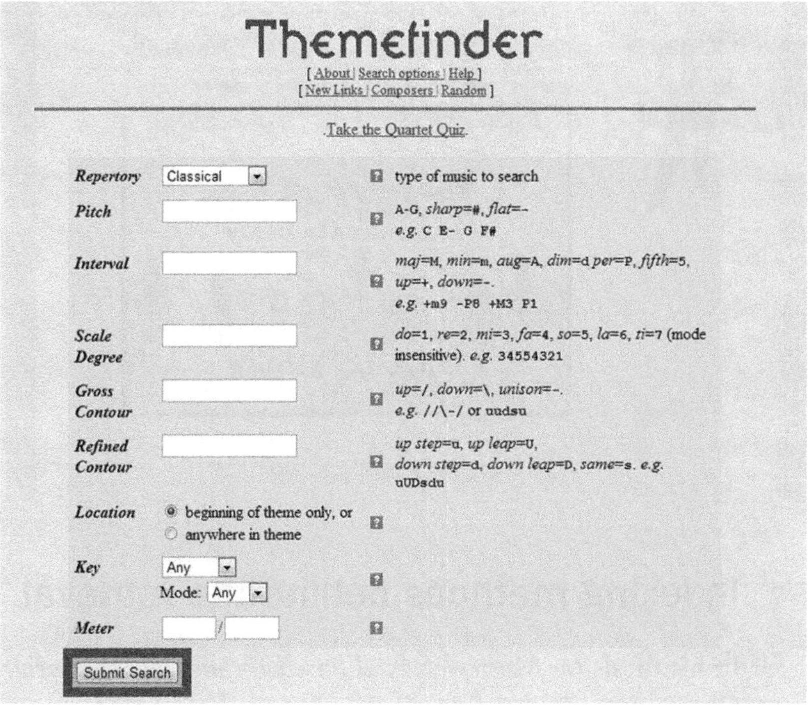

SongTapper

In SongTapper (*http://www.bored.com/songtapper/*) one can search for a song by tapping the rhythm on the spacebar, as in Figure 6.3.

Figure 6.3   SongTapper

Indexing methods behind the retrieval

In his thesis on *Music retrieval based on melodic similarity* [2], Rainer Typke lists 19 similar content-based music information retrieval sites. Some of them are commercial, some experimental sites from research institutes, but all are more or less amusing and certainly fascinating. However, we should not, once again, confuse retrieval or easiness of use with indexing techniques. An experimental music retrieval site based on very advanced indexing techniques can have an interface which is not quite user friendly because it was only meant for research purposes.

In music, different elements all go together and build the melody:

- The pitch: how high or low it sounds.
- The contour: the sequence of notes going up or down.
- The length of each note.
- Rhythm, timbre, loudness, duration of each note, etc.

In order to use these elements for indexing you will have to separate them from each other and to code them so that they can be put into a computer. You also have to find a way to divide each song in your database into minimal parts. In texts this is easy: you just take each word as a basic element. But someone who is whistling a piece of music can start and stop at any note. In order to compare this sequence to the melodies in the database you must be able to compare it to all sequences starting and stopping also at any random note, and maybe the most difficult of all may be finding a good way to calculate which part of the songs in the database match the 'question', taking into account that almost no incoming rhythm or melody will be perfect.

Typke uses a mathematical technique called 'transportation distances', which in its turn is based on the 'earth mover's distance', a technique to calculate 'the minimum amount of work needed to fill the holes with earth (measured in weight units multiplied with the covered ground distance)' [2: 30]. This technique allows him to calculate which fragment deviates the least from the searcher's entry.

A lot of research on music retrieval is reported in the annual International Conferences on Music Information

Retrieval (*http://www.ismir.net*). Most of these reports are very technical, because music indexing is far more complex than text indexing, although there are some similarities [3]:

- Text and music are both built with symbols (words or notes) which are combined according to certain rules.

- Text and music can be studied as physical phenomena, as audio signals, or in their written representations.

References

[1] Broughton, V. (2012), *Essential Library of Congress Subject Headings*. London: Facet Publishing, p. 209.

[2] Typke, R. (2007) 'Music retrieval based on melodic similarity', thesis, University of Utrecht, 15–20. Available from *http://igitur-archive.library.uu.nl/dissertations/2007-0219-200118/index.htm*

[3] Sharkra, I., Frederico, G. and El Saddik, A. (2004), 'Music indexing and retrieval', text presented at the IEE International Conference on Virtual Environments, Human Interfaces, and Measurement Systems, Boston, MD, USA, 12-14 July 2004. Available from: *http://www.elg.uottawa.ca/~elsaddik/abedweb/publications/VE-4008.pdf*

7

Taxonomies and ontologies

Classifications make strange bedfellows.
(David Weinberger [1: 90])

Abstract: Taxonomies have many appearances: they can be simple navigation lists on a website, tree structures, structured schematic representations, etc. Ontologies define relations between concepts and can be seen as a more advanced kind of thesauri. Librarians sometimes have mixed feelings regarding both: they feel that their expertise is not valued. Although taxonomies and ontologies have many applications in knowledge management, they may be used as instruments to index documents. The full power of ontologies will be realised in the Semantic Web.

Key words: ontologies, taxonomies.

The librarian's strained relation to taxonomies and ontologies

For more than a century libraries have been working with classifications, subject headings and thesauri. In the 1980s and 1990s new instruments to classify and index documents and knowledge were invented in the world of knowledge management: taxonomies and ontologies. Librarians found that taxonomies looked suspiciously similar to classifications and that ontologies were not much more than thesauri reinvented all over again. Moreover, they were not happy that the knowledge managers did not consult them and that those newcomers made such a fuss about their instruments, which the librarians considered to be just old wine in new bottles. In 1999 Dagobert Soergel published a short article which since then has been referred to many times as a typical expression of the criticism librarians have about ontologies and taxonomies [2]. He wrote:

> But a classification by any other name is still a classification. The use of a different name is symptomatic of the lack of communication between scientific communities. The vast body of knowledge on classification structure and on ways to display classifications developed around library classification and in information science more generally, and the huge intellectual capital embodied in many classification schemes and thesauri is largely ignored. Large and useful schemes are being built with more effort than necessary [2: 1120].

Others have tried to offer their services in a more positive way. An example of this attitude can be found in a 2005 article by George Plosker: 'Taxonomies: facts and opportunities for information professionals' [3]. He names six 'key project areas for which the information professional can either take the lead or add value':

1. Assist with the definition of strategic goals for the project.
2. Do needs assessments and surveys of key user groups and their information habits.
3. Select and source external taxonomies for licensing.

4. Do vendor selection by comparing and contrasting features and their relationships to needs.

5. Provide expertise in the area of knowledge management and information retrieval, including the writing and refining of indexing 'rules'.

6. Update, improve, and maintain content tools in response to new terminology, user input, and/or changes in organizational goals and directions.

The reality is that knowledge managers see all of these tasks as aspects of their core business and that they do not feel the need to ask librarians to do their jobs. In their view the librarians' approach is too limited:

■ Librarians use their instruments to classify and index documents, not to create knowledge.

■ Librarians usually do not construct classifications, thesauri etc.: they just apply them to their collection of documents.

■ Librarians still use instruments whose roots lie in the nineteenth century, where knowledge managers often need a taxonomy for one project which is limited in time; after the project the taxonomy is probably useless and replaced by something else.

■ The classical instruments of librarians, e.g. DDC or UDC, are built around a naïve philosophical view of the world and of knowledge, where knowledge managers have very different criteria: usefulness, efficiency, functionality.

This does not mean that knowledge managers do not have an open eye for a good idea, wherever it may come from. The Taxonomy Warehouse website *http://www.taxonomywarehouse.com* contains over 670 'taxonomies' meant 'to help organizations maximize their information assets and break through today's information overload'. In fact it is a collection of thesauri, subject headings, classifications, taxonomies, ontologies, glossaries, authority files, etc. To name all of these 'taxonomies' must make a librarian's grey hair stand on end. It is very illuminating to see what Taxonomy Warehouse writes on the site about some of the librarians' favourites:

- Dewey Decimal Classification: 'It is the most widely used library classification system in the world and it can be used for other purposes, such as a browsing mechanism for web information.'

- Universal Decimal Classificaton: 'The Universal Decimal Classification (UDC) is a classification scheme for all fields of knowledge and knowledge representation. It offers a logical structure to index and represent concepts, information or recorded knowledge in any form or stored in any kind of medium.'

- Library of Congress Classification: 'Classification system designed to provide bibliographic control of the Library of Congress collections. Other uses of the structure include integration of the classification and controlled subject terms for improved information storage and retrieval; organizing web resources; and generating domain-specific taxonomies.'

This gives a very good illustration of the reason why the Taxonomy Warehouse is also interested in those traditional library instruments: everything can be a starting point to building a taxonomy.

Nowadays many librarians no longer have any resentment against the fact that the borders between systems that used to be very well distinguished are fading. In her book *The Accidental Taxonomist* Heather Hedden [4] makes the distinction between taxonomies in the narrower sense (i.e. hierarchical classifications) and taxonomies in the broader sense, which could encompass glossaries, thesauri, subject headings, ontologies, etc. She clearly uses 'taxonomies' in the broader sense and a large part of her book in fact deals with thesauri. 'Thesauri', 'controlled vocabularies', 'subject headings', etc., are no longer buzzwords, whereas 'taxonomies' is, and Hedden's viewpoint seems to be that we'd better adapt ourselves to this terminology shift if we still want to participate in the game:

> It sometimes seems as if all taxonomies these days are enterprise taxonomies, because 1) it is true that most new taxonomies are indeed enterprise taxonomies, and 2) taxonomies that are not created for an enterprise are less likely to be called taxonomies but rather thesauri or controlled vocabularies. A greater number of new and planned taxonomy projects are for enterprises, simply because that is where the greatest market is.

As the proverb says, who pays the piper calls the tune . . .

What are taxonomies and what are they used for?

In classical library science a taxonomy would be a hierarchical tree structure, a classification without the codes, without the notation part. Taxonomy builders are far more flexible in their definition of what a taxonomy can be. For Patrick Lamb, author of a well-regarded book on taxonomies and knowledge management, any form of arrangement of words or concepts may be a taxonomy. He discusses seven kinds [5]:

1. Lists, i.e. collections of related things, from shopping lists to whatever scientific or administrative lists.

2. Tree structures: lists that progress from general to specific or from whole to part.

3. Hierarchies: a specific kind of tree structure. Although hierarchies have different definitions in different sciences they have in common that they are tree structures based on more rigid rules.

4. Polyhierarchies, which are created when items belong to more than one hierarchy at once.

5. Matrices: tables in which items are subscribed by their specific place, which is the intersection between two or more qualities.

6. Facets: a set of aspects by which different items may be qualified.

7. System maps: mappings, schematic representations.

Librarians are trained to use lists (e.g. of subject headings), tree structures (their classifications and thesauri) and facets. Since the days of Ranganathan, facets have been a must in library education, but they are seldom applied in library practice. The success of Ranganathan's Colon Classification [6], based on this theory of facets, is very much limited to its country of origin, India.

Taxonomies are browse instruments. If we take a look at *http://www.dmoz.org*, the largest web directory in the world, we find a tree structure built in a topical way, from general to specific. If you want to find British websites dealing with bowling, you have to descend these branches:

Sports

    Bowling

        Regional

           United Kingdom

Of course, if you know that something like *http://www. lakeside-superbowl.co.uk/* exists, you could also find it directly by entering the words 'lakeside' and 'superbowl' in the search box. This is, again, a matter of interface. The DMOZ interface offers two search possibilities, based on two different indexing methods:

1. Keyword searching, probably based on word indexing of all the URL names.

2. Browsing through the tree structure.

Almost every website contains some kind of taxonomy, mostly in the form of a list of pages that can be found on the website, but, again, this may be only one of the search possibilities, and thus only one of the indexing techniques applied on that website. For librarians, books on a certain subject can only be located in one place on the shelves, and by consequence they can only be found in one spot on the classification scheme. If a reader wants to locate a book by browsing through the stacks or through the classification scheme, he or she should take the trouble of gaining some insight into the logic behind that classification.

A taxonomy has a different view in this respect. A commercial site wants its (potential) clients to find what they are looking for regardless what kind of approach they are starting from. Sports outfit may be found starting form:

Sports

      Cycling

           Clothes

or from:

Clothes

      Sports

           Cycling

In fact, this solves one of the fundamental problems of library classifications, i.e. the phenomenon of 'distributed relatives'. However you build your classification, some subjects will be scattered all over it. In the above examples, either clothing or sports are 'distributed' because other aspects of these subjects are in totally different places. This has been one of the reasons librarians were no longer happy with their traditional classifications by the end of last century. In some countries this dissatisfaction led to the invention and introduction of new classifications for public libraries. The oddity may be that, although every book on classification theory discusses distributed relatives, the opponents and critics of traditional library classification describe the disadvantages of distributed relatives in the long and wide, but almost never use the term itself. This is still the case, as noted in David Weinberger's book *Everything is Miscellaneous*. He writes:

> The Dewey Decimal Classification system lets patrons stroll through the collected works of What We Know – our collective memory palace – exploring knowledge the way they explore a new city. But the price for ordering knowledge in the physical world is having to make either/or decisions – ironically, a characteristic more often associated with the binary nature of the digital world. The military music book is shelved with the military books or with the music books, but it can't go with both. The library's geography of knowledge can have one shape but no other. That's not a law of knowledge. It's a law of physical geography [7: 57].

Yes, we know, it is called 'distributed relatives', and it has to be said: a taxonomy can overcome this, simply by assigning items to as many branches of the tree structure as necessary.

It is not difficult to find examples of the taxonomy types Lamb defines, except maybe for the one based on facets. Good examples of a faceted structure are used car websites. On *http://www.autoweb.co.uk* the user can enter no less than nine facets:

3. make

4. model

5. age

6. body style (hatchback, convertible, van, etc.)

7. minimum price

8. maximum price

9. location of seller

10. kind of gearbox (any, manual or automatic)

11. kind of fuel (any, petrol, diesel).

This means that each used car entered into the database must be described in at least eight facets (minimum price and maximum price are in fact calculated from one facet, i.e. price).

But let us not forget that although our main interest here is the role taxonomies play in indexing, for knowledge managers they are not only tools to index documents. They are, first and foremost, a tool to get a grip on knowledge, work processes, etc. Documents usually have a function in this, because they store, describe that knowledge and play an important part in communication, but in most cases they are considered to be of subsidiary importance.

Marjorie Hlava lists the 'top 10 reasons to create a taxonomy' to show businesses why they could benefit from taxonomies [8]:

1. Searches on your website or database yield an avalanche of irrelevant returns.

2. Every person or department uses a different term, even though they're all talking about the same thing.

3. You know there's a perfect search term for what you're looking for, but you can't remember it.

4. A co-worker just spent 45 minutes trying to locate a document, but he didn't know what term to use.

5. Your masterpiece report remains undiscovered because it does not fit neatly into any of the usual research topics.

6. Six people use six different spellings or punctuations of a term, so none of them can find what they're looking for.

7. You have controlled vocabulary terms for left-handed widgets; unfortunately, you need to find reports on right-handed widgets.

8. Everything for HR gets called 'HR' ... all 10 000 documents.

9. Your website visitors keep searching on 'bumbershoots' and 'brollies'; forecasts for your umbrella department sales are gloomy.

10. People ignore your term list because it looks like a shopping list.

Some of these arguments could also apply to other traditional library instruments like subject headings (which take care of synonyms, variant spellings, etc.) or classifications (which offer structured lists for browsing through a knowledge domain from general to more specific), etc. Does this mean that we should agree with Sorgel that a classification by another name is still a classification and that all the fuss about taxonomies is unnecessary? Not quite; knowledge managers have found a way to make a new mixture of those traditional instruments and present them in a language that businesses can understand; that is very well summarized in what Hlava writes: 'The bottom line is that a good taxonomy can save your staff time, and your organization time and money' [9].

Ontologies

Ontologies are often mentioned together with taxonomies, and in fact there is a lot of confusion between these two concepts, not the least because ontologies normally contain, yes, a taxonomy. In fact it is simple: a taxonomy is (more or less) comparable to a classification and an ontology may be compared with a thesaurus. But in an ontology one can define one's own relations. Where the relations in a thesaurus are pretty much limited to 'broader term', 'narrower term' and 'related term', in an ontology you can define a relation like:

- John *has a brother* Tom.
- *Ann is working in* London.
- The book *has the title* 'In the Name of the Rose'.
- Andrew *owns a* car – and: that car *has the make* Volvo.

Unlike thesauri, ontologies are not meant primarily to index documents; their main purpose is to determine relations between concepts. The terminology may have some variations: an ontology deals with:

- Classes (also called: 'concepts') and subclasses.
- Attributes of classes and subclasses (also called 'slots', 'roles', 'properties').
- Restrictions on attributes (also called 'facets', 'registrations on slots', 'role restrictions').

- 'Instances' (items) belonging to the classes or subclasses.

Although the ontology builder is not restricted to a few predefined relation types as the thesaurus builder is, this does not mean that anything goes in ontology building. A lot of effort has been put into designing ontology languages, i.e. sets of rules on how to build an ontology. By the turn of the century a few ontology languages competed with each other:

- The Knowledge Interchange Format (KIF): *http://www-ksl.stanford.edu/knowledge-sharing/kif/*

- Simple HTML Ontology Extensions (SHOE): *http://www.cs.umd.edu/projects/plus/SHOE/onts/base.html*

- The Ontology Inference Layer (OIL): *http://www.ontoknowledge.org/oil/*

- The Defence Advanced Research Agency ontology language (DAML-ONT): *http://www.daml.org/2000/10/daml-ont.html*, and its successor:

- DAML+OIL: *http://www.daml.org/2001/03/daml+oil-index.html*

- The ABC Ontology and Model: *http://metadata.net/harmony/JODI_Final.pdf*

Some of them are still successful. In the beginning of this century the World Wide Web Consortium (*http://www.w3.org*) developed its own ontology language, the Web Ontology Language (OWL).[1] This makes OWL not just another ontology language, but a cornerstone in a huge plan to build the 'Semantic Web', also called 'Web 3.0'. It has explicit relations to the other building stones of Web 3.0: XML, RDF, etc., and for that reason it will probably become the de facto ontology standard.

In fact OWL is not one ontology language, but a set of three sublanguages:

- OWL Lite, the light version. OWL Lite is designed for basic needs and could be used to convert thesauri and taxonomies into ontologies.

- OWL DL, for 'those users who want the maximum expressiveness while retaining computational completeness' (DL does not stand for 'de luxe', but for 'description logics').

- OWL Full, a version that allows more freedom for the ontology builder, but without the guarantee that everything created will also be understandable to automatic reasoning, the ultimate goal of the web of the future.

Some basic concepts in OWL are:

- Class: a group of individuals sharing a number of properties ('thing' is defined as the main class of all).

- Subclass: a subdivision of a class.

- Property: a relationship between individuals or between individuals and other data. Properties are expressed in the so-called 'camel back notation', e.g. hasChild, hasTitle.

- Domain: defines in which class a property can be used.

- Range: limits the individuals the property can be applied to.

- Individual: an instance of a class.

Already in the first sentence of the OWL Recommendation it is stated that the 'OWL Web Ontology Language is designed for use by applications that need to process the content of information instead of just presenting information to humans' [10]. The final goal of the Semantic Web is a web in which machines can understand the content of the documents in order to decide if this content is relevant to be used as part of the answer to the question the searcher formulates. The role of ontologies in this is to 'formally describe the meaning of terminology used in web documents'. Although the W3 text puts heavy emphasis on machine readability, the whole point of the Web 3.0 instruments is that humans can read them as well as computers. Ontologies may be extracted semi-automatically from texts, or even fully automatically in future, but for now ontologies are written by humans. For that purpose ontology editors are used. They have different advantages:

- They help the ontology builder to apply the complex rules, restrictions etc.
- They can translate an ontology into a taxonomy and into an XML file.
- They can read other ontologies in XML form. These can then be used to create one's own ontology.

One of the most successful ontology editors today is without doubt the Protégé Editor (Figure 7.1), and the fact

Figure 7.1 The Protégé editor

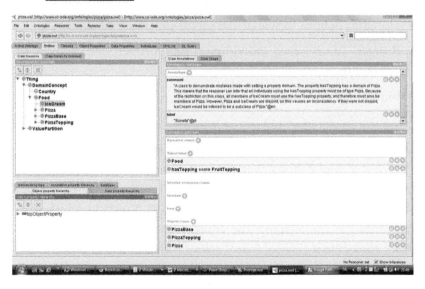

that it is a free and open source one probably has a lot to do with that. Protégé is a project of Stanford University (*http://protege.stanford.edu/*); at this moment more than 100 000 Protégé users are registered. Protégé has many extensions and plug-ins that can be used together with the standard editor; one of them is an OWL editor.

Although an editor makes it easier (or should we say more feasible?) to create an ontology, it would save a lot of work if we could reuse an already existing ontology and simply adapt it slightly to our needs. In fact, this can already be done and many sites list ontologies, but the most important tool to locate one is probably Swoogle (*http://swoogle.umbc.edu*). This ontology search engine (Figure 7.2), which has nothing to with Google except for

Figure 7.2   The Swoogle search engine

ontology   document   term   across ontologies

Swoogle Search

Searching over 10,000 ontologies

manual o news o faq o web-service o submit-url o sw-archive o feedback o swoogle2005

Swoogle ® 2004-2007, ebiquity group at UMBC
This work is licensed under a Creative Commons Attribution-NonCommercial-ShareAlike 2.5 License.

the intentional resemblance in its looks, contains more than 10 000 ontologies in XML form.

A search in Swoogle will lead to a list of ontologies on a certain subject, as in Figure 7.3. A click on a link will normally display the ontology in XML format, but Swoogle also offers many instruments to get more information on each of the ontologies and a few tools to get a comprehensive overview of them. One of those tools makes it possible to display the class hierarchy, i.e. the taxonomy, which forms the backbone of the ontology (see Figure 7.4).

It is surprising to see that, although the main goal of ontologies is to make it possible for computer programs

Figure 7.3 Results of a search in Swoogle

Figure 7.4   Hierarchical display of an ontology in Swoogle

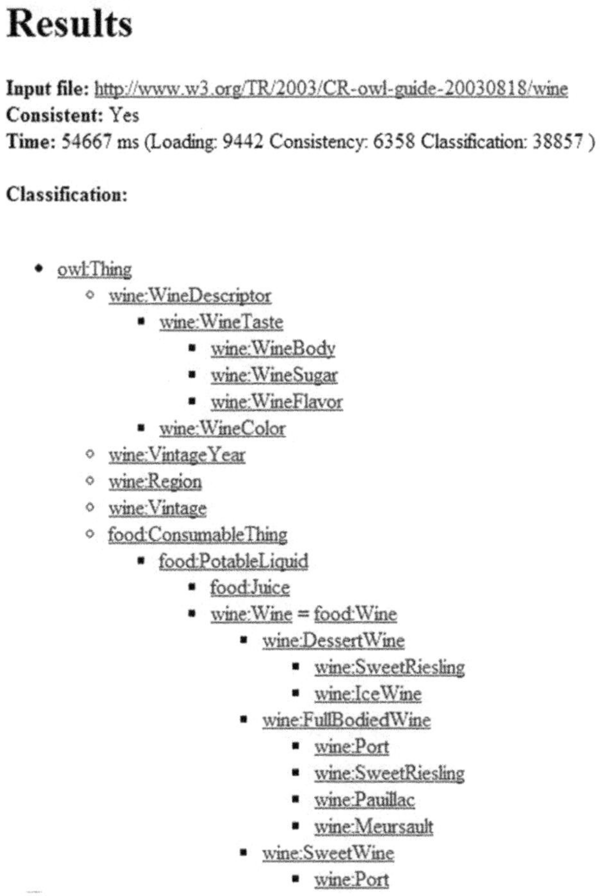

Results

Input file: http://www.w3.org/TR/2003/CR-owl-guide-20030818/wine
Consistent: Yes
Time: 54667 ms (Loading: 9442 Consistency: 6358 Classification: 38857)

Classification:

- owl:Thing
  - wine:WineDescriptor
    - wine:WineTaste
      - wine:WineBody
      - wine:WineSugar
      - wine:WineFlavor
    - wine:WineColor
  - wine:VintageYear
  - wine:Region
  - wine:Vintage
  - food:ConsumableThing
    - food:PotableLiquid
      - food:Juice
      - wine:Wine = food:Wine
        - wine:DessertWine
          - wine:SweetRiesling
          - wine:IceWine
        - wine:FullBodiedWine
          - wine:Port
          - wine:SweetRiesling
          - wine:Pauillac
          - wine:Meursault
        - wine:SweetWine
          - wine:Port

to understand and process the information in web files, a lot of effort was put into the development of tools that can perform a graphical display of an ontology – whose sole purpose is to make it more intelligible for humans. An example can be found at *http://www.inoh.org/ontology-viewer* (Figure 7.5).

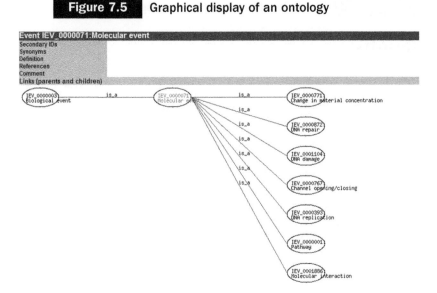

Figure 7.5   Graphical display of an ontology

The importance of taxonomies and ontologies

In her famous article, 'Ontologies come of age' [11], Deborah McGuinness gives an overview of possible uses for ontologies and taxonomies.[2] She makes a distinction between 'simple ontologies' and 'structured ontologies'. For simple ontologies (and taxonomies) she names seven possible uses:

1. As a controlled vocabulary: if many users accept the same controlled vocabulary interoperability becomes easier.

2. As a tool for site organization and navigation: website builders can use a taxonomy to structure their site.

3. To support expectation setting: if a user explores the taxonomy of a website he will be able to decide quickly if that website contains any relevant information.

4. As 'umbrella' structures from which you can start to extend content. This means that if you have a good structure, i.e. a good taxonomy, it is easy to create a subclass in which new information can be located.

5. Taxonomies can be browsing supports – which is complementary to number two: if a site is built upon a taxonomy, the user will of course navigate through the site by clicking the different buttons, i.e. the classes and subclasses.

6. Taxonomies may be used to provide search support: we can explore the categories of a taxonomy in order to find more specific terms that can be used as search terms.

7. They can be used to sense disambiguation support. McGuinness gives the example of 'Jordan', a homonym which can refer to either a country or a famous basketball player. The place of 'Jordan' in the taxonomy (as an instance of 'countries' or as an instance of 'basketball players') reveals which 'Jordan' is meant.

For 'structured ontologies' McGuiness finds eight uses:

1. For consistency checking: if something belongs to a certain class, it must have the properties of that class, and if it does not have these properties it should not be categorized into this class.

2. To provide completion: if we know to which class something belongs we know which properties it has.

3. To provide interoperability support: if we use the same taxonomy or ontology as others, it will be easier to exchange information with them.

4. To support validation and verification testing of data: we can use the relations built into a well structured

ontology to check if the relations in a given database are consistent.

5. To encode entire test suites, which is almost the same as number 4, but now applied to a knowledge management system.

6. For configuration support: the relations between classes, subclasses, instances and their restrictions can be used as a reference when we want to program an application for a complex situation, e.g. an e-commerce site.

7. To support structured, comparative and customized searches: the detailed relations in an ontology can make it easier to compare details in the results of searches based on ontologies, provided that we have search engines based on ontologies. If we want to compare the details in the results from 'normal' search engines, we have to read through each entire document and evaluate the information in it; a search engine based on an ontology could do this for us.

8. To exploit generalization/specialization information: a search engine using an ontology could suggest terms to make the search more specific (if too many answers are found) or to make it more general (if not enough answers are found).

Although many of these 15 types of uses seem to be complicated, the moral of the story is quite simple: ontologies and taxonomies can be very good instruments for structuring data, and as a consequence, also for searching and comparing data. Up until now, many applications have been built that use one or more aspects of ontologies and taxonomies, but their full power will be released when the Semantic Web is realized. This may still take some time, as we will see in Chapter 12.

Notes

1. It beats me why the acronym for 'Web Ontology Language' is 'OWL'. Is it because the owl is the symbol of wisdom?
2. The article deals with ontologies, but the author does not make a clear distinction between ontologies and taxonomies in this part of her text (McGuinness, D.L. 'Ontologies come of age', in: Fensel, D., Hendler, J., Lieberman, H. and Wahlster, W. (eds) (2003), *Spinning the Semantic Web: Bringing the World Wide Web to its Full Potential*. Cambridge, MA: MIT Press, 178–85).

References

[1] Weinberger, D. (2007), *Everything is Miscellaneous: the Power of the New Digital Disorder*. New York: Holt.

[2] Soergel, D. (1999), 'The rise of ontologies or the reinvention of classification', *Journal of the American Society for Information Science*, 50: 1119–20.

[3] Plosker, G. (2005), 'Taxonomies: facts and opportunities for information professionals', *Online*, 29, 1: 59–60.

[4] Hedden, H. (2010), *The Accidental Taxonomist*. Medford, NJ: Information Today, p. 303.

[5] Lamb, P. (2007), *Organising Knowledge: Taxonomies, Knowledge and Organisational Effectiveness*. Oxford: Chandos, 13–48.

[6] Ranganathan, S.R. (2006), *Colon Classification* (sixth edition). New Delhi: Ess Ess Publications.

[7] Weinberger, D. (2007), *Everything is Miscellaneous: the Power of the New Digital Disorder*. New York: Holt.

[8] Hlava, M.M.K. (2011), 'The top 10 reasons to create a taxonomy', *Information Today*, 28, 2: 21.

[9] Ibid.

[10] McGuinness, D.L. and Van Harmelen, F. (2004), 'OWL Web Ontology Language overview'. Available from: *http://www.w3.org/TR/owl-features/*

[11] McGuinness, D.L. (2003), 'Ontologies come of age', in: Fensel, D., Hendler, J., Lieberman, H. and Wahlster, W. (eds) (2003), *Spinning the Semantic Web: Bringing the World Wide Web to its Full Potential*. Cambridge, MA: MIT Press, 171–222.

8

Metadata formats and indexing

There's just no getting away from rules and standards in this line of work.

(Deborah and Richard Fritz [1])

Abstract: This chapter gives an overview of the most important metadata formats and the way they treat subject indexing. Libraries used to be the primary source of structured metadata, but in the last decades of the twentieth century new standards successfully emerged in different environments and also made their way into the library world. Some metadata formats provide facilities to store detailed and structured subject information; others leave a lot of freedom to the user. The multitude of formats make conversion from one into another necessary, which may result in loss of structure. Specific instruments were developed to transfer data from one format into another: frameworks, registers and crosswalks.

Key words: metadata formats, metadata frameworks, metadata registries, metadata crosswalks.

Introduction

In this chapter we will give an overview of different metadata schemes that have some connection with the library world and we will point out what their relation to indexing is.

Although metadata schemes may be considered to be an issue for the cataloguing section, which deals with the formal aspects of documents, they are of great importance for indexing. A metadata scheme defines which information about a document will be recorded and in which way. This also applies to information about the content of a document. In Chapter 12 we will see how structured data is fundamental for the future of indexing.

What are metadata?

Each book, each article, each chapter on metadata formats must start with the question 'What are metadata?' A definition of metadata may be as simple as 'metadata are data about data' or as complex as the one David Haynes gives in his book *Metadata for Information Management and Retrieval*, after analysing many definitions he found in the literature:

> Metadata is data that describes the content, formats or attributes of a data record or information resource. It can be used to describe highly structured resources or unstructured information such as text documents. Metadata can be applied to description of: electronic resources; digital data (including digital images); and to printed documents such as books, journals and reports. Metadata can be embedded within the information resource (as is often the case with web resources) or it can be held separately in a database [2].

In his book on *Metadata for Digital Collections*, Stephen J. Miller does not try to correct or complete this and other definitions; he just points out the main characteristics of metadata [3]:

- Metadata consist of a set of properties (elements or fields) and a set of values for each property.
- Metadata stand apart from the information resource they are about.
- They are grouped together in a record.

As metadata now take many forms, this kind of approach may well be more pragmatic than trying to cram in more in an already oversized definition.

Metadata and the library world

Creating metadata was always part of library work and a list of books in the library of Alexandria must in fact have been one of the first 'metadata files'. A lot of effort was invested in standardization of (traditional) library metadata in the 1960s and 1970s, which resulted in a whole set of rules for the bibliographic description of books and other media, the International Standard Bibliographic Description (ISBD) rules. At the same time, Machine-Readable Cataloguing (MARC) formats were developed. Since then, both, MARC and ISBD have been taught at length in library schools.

In the 1990s a whole new situation was created in regard to the way documents were stored and distributed, and by consequence the 'old' metadata standards did not meet with the new needs – although adjustments were made in the light of new document forms, e.g. websites. The rapid changes in this field are well illustrated if we compare the contents of a few publications on metadata standards. In 1990, at the dawn of the World Wide Web, Ellen Gredley and Alan Hopkinson published a very good book on MARC and other international standards for the exchange of bibliographic data [4]; nothing in it refers to the Internet at this time and it may have been the final book on metadata standards of the pre-web period.

In an article of 1996, Rachel Heery gave an overview of some important metadata formats and discussed, among others MARC, IAFA/WHOIS++ Templates, the Text Encoding Initiative (TEI) headers, Uniform Resource Characteristics (URCs) and Dublin Core, which was new and hot at that time [5]. Books published by the turn of the century, e.g. Priscilla Caplan's *Metadata Fundamentals for All Librarians* [6] have to deal with XML and give an overview of a dozen standards,[1] e.g.

- Dublin Core (DC)
- Text Encoding Initiative (TEI)
- Metadata Encoding and Transmission Standard (METS)
- Metadata Object Description Schema (MODS)
- Encoded Archive Description (EAD)
- Gateway to Educational Materials (GEM)
- Learning Object Metadata (LOM)
- Online Information Exchange Standard (ONIX)
- Categories for the Description of Works of Art (CDWA)
- Visual Resources Association Core Categories (VRA Core)
- MPEG-7 and MPEG-21.

Unlike MARC or ISBD, most of these standards have not been designed for the library world, but libraries may apply them one way or another and therefore librarians should at least have some notion of them.

Some important metadata standards

Daniel Chudnov, Information Technology Specialist at the Library of Congress, writes: 'It's been said that "the great thing about standards is that there are so many to choose from". It's also been said that "if you like laws, sausages, and standards, do not watch them being made" ' [7]. Indeed, many standards and variations to other standards exist and each standard in itself is very technical. It would lead us too far to discuss each one at length, but without a brief overview of some of them the importance and relevance of metadata standards for indexing cannot be shown.

Dublin Core

Dublin Core[2] – or 'the Dublin Core Metadata Element Set', as its full name officially sounds – was created as a result of a congress in Dublin, Ohio, in 1995, in order to address the need for a relatively simple and easy way to add structured metadata to web pages. Since then it has been the mother of many modern metadata formats and it gained the status of both an ISO and a NISO standard.[3] Dublin Core (DC) defines 15 basic elements to describe a document:

1. Title
2. Creator
3. Subject
4. Description
5. Publisher
6. Contributor
7. Date
8. Type
9. Format
10. Identifier
11. Source

12. Language

13. Relation

14. Coverage

15. Rights

These elements form the classic DC, which now evolved to a more complex metadata scheme with 55 'metadata terms'.

DC leaves a lot of freedom, and the question could be asked if it does not leave too much room for this freedom. For 'Creator', DC gives this explanation: 'Examples of a Creator include a person, an organization, or a service. Typically, the name of a Creator should be used to indicate the entity.' This does not say how this element should be filled in. Which of these possibilities is the best?

John Smith

Smith, John

Smith John

%aSmith%bJohn
Etc.

For other elements a suggestion is given, e.g. for 'Date': 'recommended best practice is to use an encoding scheme, such as the W3CDTF profile of ISO 8601 [W3CDTF]', and for the element 'Subject', DC gives this advice: 'Typically, the subject will be represented using keywords, key phrases, or classification codes. Recommended best practice is to use a controlled vocabulary.'

In one case, namely for the element 'Type', the Dublin Core Metadata Initiative (DCMI) developed its own vocabulary but here, too, one is only recommended to use it. This policy may allow as much freedom as possible, while at the same time it provides a tool to bring uniformity and structure into what otherwise would be a very chaotic world of unstructured documents, but it is not without consequences for indexing.

DC was a very important milestone in the world of indexing. Indexing was no longer the sole domain of the (library) professional; everybody who knew how to create a web page had the tools to index it in a structured and standardized way by adding DC values in the head of the web page, e.g. <meta name='DC.date' content='2011-07-21' />.

Internet search engines could then read this information and store it in their databases. The only problem with this way of describing your own web page is that it has become totally useless. Very soon it was realized that the metatags in Hypertext Markup Language (HTML) could be used for deceiving search engines by accumulating popular search terms in it; anyone who is using for these popular subjects will be confronted with every web page that contains it, although it deals with totally different things, e.g. pornography. Consequently, the value of DC no longer lies in its use for the metatags. It now is more important as a field structure for many kinds of databases, especially for 'open archives', because of the relative simplicity of its structure.

Metadata Standard for Electronic Theses and Dissertations (ETD-MS)

A standard that is very close to DC is the ETD-MS standard which is used for electronic archives of theses at universities and other educational institutes. The original DC field structure was slightly modified to apply to the specific needs of those archives:

1. dc.title
2. dc.creator
3. dc.subject

4. dc.description

5. dc.publisher

6. dc.contributor

7. dc.date

8. dc.type

9. dc.format

10. dc.identifier

11. dc.language

12. dc.coverage

13. dc.rights

14. thesis.degree

The last element can be subdivided into a few others:

- thesis.degree.name
- thesis.degree.level
- thesis.degree.discipline
- theses.degree.grantor

This metadata format is now popular in many repositories of Masters' and other theses in the world. Most of those repositories are filled in by the students themselves, with or without corrections made afterwards by library personnel. One of the problems is that the format is relatively open, i.e. students can e.g. fill in anything in the field for 'Subject'. Some studies into the quality of the data have been conducted in recent years. The main question of these studies is what is the balance between quality and costs? If we want to correct all errors we need to invest in trained personnel, but if we want to save costs we need to find a way to get the quality of the metadata to an acceptable level without interference from expensive personnel. There has been a similar discussion about the relation between costs and quality of metadata in traditional library cataloguing, although from a different angle. The main issue there was can we do without controlled vocabularies and rely on keywords extracted from title, etc.?

MARC21

MARC21 is still the leading metadata format in cataloguing. Since the beginning of this century MARC21 is being revised. MARC21 was based upon AACRII, the Anglo-American Cataloguing Rules second edition, and as AACRII itself has been updated to its third edition, now called Resource Description and Access (RDA), MARC21 had to follow. At this moment the Library of Congress is investigating how to implement RDA in its catalogues. The classical MARC21 will still be with us for some time, if only because many library cataloguing software packages will need years to adapt to the new situation.

As always, a new version of such important standards has provoked a lot of emotional reactions. For some, the world (of cataloguing) is coming to an end. In 2007 Michael Gorman, the spiritual father of ISBD, wrote that he considered RDA to be 'the biggest disaster to hit descriptive cataloging since the draft rules of 1941' [8] – which is a very strong statement, since the draft rules of 1941 are considered to be the biggest fiasco in the world of cataloguing standards ever.

MARC21 has many fields in which subjects can be entered according to their nature:

600 – Subject Added Entry – Personal Name

610 – Subject Added Entry – Corporate Name

611 – Subject Added Entry – Meeting Name

630 – Subject Added Entry – Uniform Title

648 – Subject Added Entry – Chronological Term

650 – Subject Added Entry – Topical Term

651 – Subject Added Entry – Geographic Name

653 – Index Term – Uncontrolled

654 – Subject Added Entry – Faceted Topical Terms

655 – Index Term – Genre/Form

656 – Index Term – Occupation

657 – Index Term – Function

658 – Index Term – Curriculum Objective

662 – Subject Added Entry – Hierarchical Place Name

69X – Local Subject Access Fields

The well-known technique of indicators allows the recording of from which controlled vocabulary the term was taken.

If we accept that classifications also tell something about the content of a document, even more fields, now in the 0XX range, should also be considered as subject fields:

050 – Library of Congress Call Number

051 – Library of Congress Copy, Issue, Offprint Statement

052 – Geographic Classification

055 – Classification Numbers Assigned in Canada

060 – National Library of Medicine Call Number

061 – National Library of Medicine Copy Statement

066 – Character Sets Present

070 – National Agricultural Library Call Number

071 – National Agricultural Library Copy Statement

072 – Subject Category Code

074 – GPO Item Number

080 – Universal Decimal Classification Number

082 – Dewey Decimal Classification Number

083 – Additional Dewey Decimal Classification Number

084 – Other Classification Number

085 – Synthesized Classification Number Components

086 – Government Document Classification Number

It has to be said that the role of classifications in library catalogues is ambiguous. Some classifications, e.g. the Universal Decimal Classification (UDC), was clearly developed to express the subject of documents in every detail, but it is now used as a tool to create shelf numbers which most library users just regard as coding for the exact spot where they can find a book. MARC also has a special format for authority files:

100 – Heading – Personal Name

110 – Heading – Corporate Name

111 – Heading – Meeting Name

130 – Heading – Uniform Title

148 – Heading – Chronological Term

150 – Heading – Topical Term

151 – Heading – Geographic Name

155 – Heading – Genre/Form Term

180 – Heading – General Subdivision

181 – Heading – Geographic Subdivision

182 – Heading – Chronological Subdivision

185 – Heading – Form Subdivision

All this shows that MARC is a professional but very complicated format. It leaves room for every kind of controlled vocabulary or classification, as well as for uncontrolled terms, and it offers a structure that can make a clear distinction between each kind. The 'classical' MARC now has an XML version, but besides that some special metadata formats have been created that translate MARC into simplified XML schemes.

Metadata Object Description Schema (MODS)

MODS is related to MARC21 and maintained by the Network Development and MARC Standards Office of the Library of Congress.[4] MODS uses alphanumeric fields, which makes a MODS record more readable than a MARC one. The official MODS website lists four advantages of MODS to a few other standards:

- The element set is richer than DC.
- The element set is more compatible with library data than ONIX.
- The schema is more end-user oriented than the full MARCXML schema.
- The element set is simpler than the full MARC format [9].

MODS Lite is a simplified version that has only fields that correspond with the 15 DC elements.

As well as MARC, MODS allows storing controlled terms, uncontrolled terms and classification codes, e.g.

<subject authority='lcsh'>

<topic>Journalism</topic>

<topic>Political aspects</topic>

<geographic>United States.</geographic>

</subject>

<classification authority='lcc'>PN4888.P6 A48 1999 </classification>

<classification edition='21' authority='ddc'>071/.3 </classification>

The Metadata Authority Description Schema (MADS) has the same purpose as the MARC authority format.

Metadata Encoding and Transmission Standard (METS)

METS[5] originated from the 'Making of America' project, 'a digital library of primary sources in American social history from the antebellum period through reconstruction' [10], i.e. a collection of texts mainly from the nineteenth century. These texts were digitalized and published in an image and a text format. METS was created as a standard to structure the administrative documentation on each document. METS has seven sections, all containing another kind of information. Section five, for instance, outlines the hierarchal structure of the document. Like TEI, METS also has a header containing metadata about the METS documents itself, while another part gives a bibliographic description of the digitized document. A METS document consists of seven parts:

1. The METS header: the description of the document itself.

2. Descriptive metadata, e.g. a reference to a MARC record in a library catalogue.

3. Administrative metadata: a description of the origin of the document, copyrights, etc.

4. The file section: a list of all parts that together build the document.

5. An overview of the hierarchical structure of the document.

6. A description of the links in the document, e.g. links from one chapter to another.

7. The behaviour section: reference to an executable code, e.g. if the document at hand is a video it can play with this code.

METS integrates parts of other standards: DC, MARCXML and MODS. It does not offer tools for subject indexing; this should be done in the descriptive metadata by taking metadata elements from other standards.

Text Encoding Initiative (TEI)

TEI[6] is older than DC: it was developed at the beginning of the 1990s. It is a set of codes that can be used to create and publish electronic versions of texts. In fact, it is an instrument for philologists who study and publish old texts. They are interested in small textual variants, the history of them, comments made in other text editions, etc. TEI lets them encode all of this. The TEI website states: 'Since 1994, the TEI Guidelines have been widely used by libraries, museums, publishers, and individual scholars to present texts for online research, teaching, and preservation.' The website gives a list of more than 100 projects using TEI.

Technically it is a Standard Generalized Markup Language (SGML) application, similar to HTML. Strictly speaking a text coded in TEI is not metadata, except for the so-called *teiheader*, a part of the document which contains metadata about the TEI document itself and about the text that is coded in it. The *teiheader* allows us to record keywords, terms from controlled vocabularies or classifications, e.g.

<keywords scheme=#lcsh>

<list>

<item>Bohemianism.</item>

<item>English literature – Nineteenth century – History and criticism.</item>

</list>

</keywords>

and

<classCode schema='#ddc>811.3</classCode>

Metadata schemes for educational materials: GEM, LOM and DC-ED

The Gateway to Education Materials (GEM) and the Learning Object Metadata (LOM) were developed to describe educational materials on the web. GEM basically uses the DC elements, but it has also some new ones which can be used to record specific information on how the resource can be applied in education.[7] LOM is a product of the Learning Technology Standards Committee, which produces and accredits standards for e-learning.[8] Like GEM it also allows you to record information on the use of the described item in educational situations.

LOM has nine categories of metadata:

1. General
2. Lifecycle
3. Meta-Metadata
4. Technical
5. Educational
6. Rights
7. Relation

8. Annotation

9. Classification

The category 'General' contains the following sections among others:

1.4 Description

1.5 Keyword

1.6 Coverage: information about time, culture, place, etc.

Only with 1.6 is the use of a controlled vocabulary recommended, e.g. the *Thesaurus of Geographic Names*. In the section 'Classification' it is possible to record terms from classifications. In the DC family, the Dublin Core Education Application Profile (DC-ED) is meant for the description of educational materials. The DC-ED Community is still investigating suitable vocabularies to recommend to the users.

The Online Information Exchange International Standard (ONIX)

ONIX[9] originates from the bookselling industry and should be an instrument in the communication between booksellers and libraries. Theoretically, libraries could get bibliographic descriptions about books and journals from the bookseller, and process them into their catalogues. ONIX has two versions: 'ONIX for Books' and 'ONIX for Serials'. An ONIX record is divided into different blocks, which can contain different groups. The block <DescriptiveDetail> contains a group 'P. 12, *subject*'. In this group different subject terms from various systems can be filled in. The manual says:

> Group P.12, *subject*, allows an unlimited number of subject categories to be assigned to a product. Category

codes or headings may be taken from any of some seventy or more supported category schemes (for example, *BISAC, BIC, Dewey, Library of Congress*). The same group also allows a personal or corporate name to be specified as part of the subject of a product (for example, a biography of *Franklin D Roosevelt*), using exactly the same name format as in Group P.6. Subject detail is optional in terms of the *ONIX for Books* schema, but it is expected in most applications.[10]

CDWA and VRA

The Categories for the Description of Works of Art (CDWA)[11] and the Visual Resources Association Core Categories (VRA Core)[12] are both metadata standards for the description of works of art. CDWA, a project of the well-known Getty Museum, offers not less than 381 categories to describe a work of art. All kinds of details on materials, texture, colour, etc. can be encoded in this standard. By comparison, VRA Core is a lot more modest: it contains only 19 fields. This illustrates one of the main problems: standards can be extremely exhaustive or, on the contrary, just elementary.

In particular, CDWA allows us to go into very nuanced details about the subject side of a work of art: the 'ofness', as well as the 'aboutness', and different interpretations can be recorded. In field 16, 'Subject matter' there is room for all nuances:

16.1 Subject display: a description of the subject depicted, e.g. 'Madonna with Child in a garden'.

16.2 Subject indexing terms: terms that characterize what is depicted, e.g. 'Madonna', 'Jesus', 'garden', 'trees', 'clouds'.

16.2.1. Subject indexing type: what the work is 'of' and what it is 'about', e.g. description, interpretation.

16.2.2. Subject extent: term that indicates the part of the work to which a subject applies, e.g. recto, left panel.

16.3 Subject interpretive history.

16.4 Remarks.

16.5 Citations: references to bibliographic sources, etc.

16.5.1 Page: page numbers etc. of these references.

MPEG-7 and MPEG-21

The Moving Picture Experts Group (MPEG)[13] has many technical standards in regard to audio or visual material. MPEG-7 and MPEG-21 were developed to contain the description of audio-visual works. MPEG-7 can be considered as a metadata standard, while MPEG-21 is strictly speaking a multimedia 'framework', a kind of container built from other standards.

Bridges between standards

It seems like standard builders were overzealous in developing new standards. The aim of DC was to provide 'simple standards to facilitate the finding, sharing and management of information', as the DC website states [11]. But the problem is that 'simple' is not good enough if you want to register technical details about audio-visual recordings or if you want to describe every relevant aspect of a complex work of art.

It is very understandable that complex standards were developed in order to make it possible to encode all relevant information in a given situation or of a specific document. The downside is that this situation does not make information retrieval or data exchange any easier. To tackle this problem a few techniques can be used:

Metadata frameworks

A framework is a reference model in which existing metadata schemes can find a place. To some extent all metadata standards re-use (parts of) previous ones. Parts of DC, being of the first modern standard, are used in many more recent ones, but even DC uses – or at least suggests using – already existing standards.

Metadata crosswalks

Crosswalks are mappings between two or more standards. If you want to convert MODS data into DC, you can read which MODS field corresponds to which DC field in the 'Mods to Dublin Core Metadata Element Set Mapping' (*http://www.loc.gov/standards/mods/mods-dcsimple.html*). You will find there that the MODS fields 'dateIssued', 'dataCreated', 'dateCaptured' and 'dataOther' should all go into DC field 'Date'.

Converting MODS into DC is an example of a many-to-one conversion; the result may be less detailed, but at least the conversion is manageable. The biggest problem is to convert data from a simple standard, e.g. DC, into a more complex one. An extreme example of this may be the conversion of CDWA into other standards. The Getty Museum publishes on its website a crosswalk of CDWA into other different standards.[14] The most important crosswalks are those that map other standards to DC, as DC is the standard format for 'open archives', i.e. repositories of documents. Crosswalks come in two forms: tables which compare two or more standards and programs that can convert data stored in one standard into another format of another standard.[15]

Metadata registries

Registries are files containing very detailed information on a given standard. The purpose is to provide all necessary information to apply the standard or to understand data coded in this standard. Normally registries come in two versions: one understandable for humans and another, in XML format, meant to be usable by computer programs. An example is the DC registry hosted by the University of Tsukuba in Japan: *http://dcmi.kc.tsukuba.ac.jp/dcregistry*.

The benefits of metadata standards

Why should we invest in metadata? Why study a lot of technical details, rules on how to encode each tiny detail of information according to a standard someone else invented? Why not encode the data we really need in the way we think is best? In his book on *Metadata for Information Management and Retrieval*, David Haynes gives five functions for metadata [12]:

1. Resource description: metadata contain a description of different aspects of a resource: title, data of creation or publication, etc. That is probably the first thing we think of when the word 'metadata' is mentioned. All traditional library metadata, like ISBD or MARC, are mainly doing this.

2. Management of the information resource: metadata document organizational aspects of the resource. They tell who created it, how it changed and when, who owns it, etc.

3. Documenting ownership and authenticity of digital resource: they give information about the copyright or other legal issues connected with the document:

4. Interoperability: they allow data transfer between systems, because they structure the information about the documents.

5. Data exchange. The ultimate goal of using metadata standards is to facilitate data exchange between systems. At the moment, the most successful examples of this are harvesters based on the Open Archives Initiative Protocol for Metadata Harvesting (OAI-PMH). In order to make this possible, two conditions must be fulfilled: the repositories must follow the open archives protocol and they must be able to present their data to the visiting harvester according to the Dublin Core standard. In doing so, they can open up part of 'the deep web'.

In their book on *Metadata for Digital Resources*, Muriel Foulonneau and Jeann Riley list five basics that make metadata interchangeable [13]:

1. Sharable metadata is quality metadata.

2. Sharable metadata promotes search interoperability.

3. Sharable metadata is human understandable outside of its local context.

4. Sharable metadata is useful outside of its local context.

5. Sharable metadata preferably is machine processable.

None of this can be realized without standards.

What about indexing?

The first purpose of metadata formats still is the resource description: they allow us to record the 'formal' characteristics of documents: title, authors, publication year, etc. Most formats have one or more fields in which something about the subject, the content of a document, can be stored. Does this mean that we have to rely on the subject fields if we want metadata formats to give a role in the indexing process? It is far more complex than that.

Metadata formats do not prescribe which system should be used to describe the subject of the document at hand. They only say that if we want to tell something about the subject, we must do it in this or that field, e.g. the 'subject' field in DC, and maybe they give the suggestion that it might be a good idea to use a controlled vocabulary. But they leave it up to the user whether he should choose a widely accepted general one or a more specific one, and whether he should use an already existing specific one or invent something new. Suppose we would all agree to use the same metadata format, say DC. This would make it a lot easier to know where to search for information about the content of the document – which is one of the basic ideas behind the development of a format like DC of course. This has indeed led to the fascinating tools that open archive harvesters are. But these leave us struggling with a multitude of different more or less controlled vocabularies, and last but not least, with a multitude of languages.

A lot of effort is put into the development of metadata bridges, but it remains difficult and sometimes impossible to translate the structure of one format into another. Information might get lost if we have to convert a more complex format into a simpler one, and the richness of the format may be unused if we convert a simple format into a complex one.

OAIster [14], one of the largest harvesters in the world, now manages to offer many more fields to search than a year ago, but it still offers one fields to search for the subject of a publication. In this field one can enter any subject, in any language, according to whatever system of controlled vocabularies, e.g. LCSH. This will surely retrieve some documents, but it leaves us with the frustration of knowing that we will have missed many more.

Notes

1. Overviews of metadata standards can be found at *http://metadata.net* or *http://www.ifla.org/II/metadata.htm*
2. For details, see: *http://dublincore.org*
3. ISO 15836-2003 and NISO Z39.85-2007.
4. Documentation about MODS can be found at *http://www.loc.gov/standards/mods*
5. See *http://www.loc.gov/standards/mets*
6. See *http://www.tei-c.org*
7. See: *http://www.thegateway.org/about/documentation/metadataElements*
8. See: *http://www.ieeeltsc.org/standards*
9. For further information see *http://www.editeur.org/onix.html*
10. The ONIX manual, *ONIX for Books: Product Information Format and Introduction to ONIX 3.0*, is available from *http://www.editeur.org/files/ONIX%203/Introduction_to_ONIX_for_Books_3.0.pdf*
11. See: *http://www.getty.edu/research/conducting_research/standards/cdwa*
12. See: *http://www.vraweb.org/projects/vracore4/index.html*
13. See: *http://www.chiariglione.org/mpeg*
14. See: *http://www.getty.edu/research/conducting_research/standards/intrometadata/metadata_element_sets.html*
15. An overview of many crosswalks can be found at: *http://www.ukoln.ac.uk/metadata/interoperability*

References

[1] Fritz, D.A., Fritz, R.J. (2003), *MARC21 for Everyone: a Practical Guide*. Chicago: American Library Association, p. 11.

[2] Haynes, D. (2004), *Metadata for Information Management and Retrieval*. London: Facet Publishing, p. 8.

[3] Miller, J.S. (2011), *Metadata for Digital Collections: a How-to-do-it Manual*. London: Facet Publishing, pp. 1–6.

[4] Gredley, E. and Hopkinson, A. (1990), *Exchanging Bibliographic Data: MARC and Other International Formats*. Ottawa: Canadian Library Association.

[5] Heery, R. (1996), 'Review of metadata formats', *Program*, 30: 345–73.

[6] Caplan, P. (2003), *Metadata Fundamentals for All Librarians*. Chicago: ALA Publications.

[7] Chudnov, D. (2011), 'The mistakes we make with standards', *Computers in Libraries*, 31, 7: 29.

[8] Gorman, M. (2007), 'RDA: imminent debacle', *American Libraries*, 38, 11: 64–5.

[9] *http://www.loc.gov/standards/mods/mods-overview.html*

[10] *http://quod.lib.umich.edu/m/moagrp*

[11] *http://dublincore.org/about*

[12] Haynes, D. (2004), *Metadata for Information Management and Retrieval*. London: Facet Publishing, pp. 12–17.

[13] Foulonneau, M. and Riley, J. (2008), *Metadata for Digital Resources: Implementation, Systems Design and Interoperability*. Oxford: Chandos Publishing, pp. 176–81.

[14] *http://oaister.worldcat.org*

9

Tagging

Is it really possible that the problem of organizing and classifying can be solved as simply as allowing random users to contribute tags?

(Jason P. Morrison [1])

Abstract: Since 2003 tagging has become very popular. When studies on tagging originally wanted to point out to a new phenomenon on the web, they now try to compare it to more traditional forms of indexing and to create a taxonomy of it. Tagging has various advantages and disadvantages. Libraries have taken different initiatives to incorporate it into their catalogues: they offer the possibility to their patrons to tag the books they retrieve or they link to already tagged books on LibraryThing. Tags can be displayed in many forms, but tags clouds may be the most popular display at this moment.

Key words: tagging, Web 2.0, social bookmarking.

What is tagging?

Tagging is adding 'tags' or labels to electronic documents on the web. These can be:

- an image on a site like Flickr
- a video on a video site like YouTube
- a music clip

- the description of a book in a library catalogue
- the description of some kind of merchandise on a vendor site like Amazon
- a document in full text.

The popularity of the phenomenon came along with that of 'social sites'. Generally the year 2003 is regarded as the starting point for social sites and also for tagging. Social sites are also called 'the social web' or 'Web 2.0', as opposed to 'Web 1.0', which is the 'web of documents', the web as we have known it since its beginning in 1989–1990.

A lot of attention has been given to tagging as a social phenomenon, as a way of social interaction. Up until a few years ago the articles that were published about tagging just wanted to draw attention to this new phenomenon. Even the first book about it, *Tagging: People-Powered Metadata for the Social Web* by Gene Smith [2], was basically of the same nature. Meanwhile more thorough studies were written, e.g. *Folksonomies: Indexing and Retrieval in Web 2.0* by Isabelle Peters [3], undoubtedly the most complete book on tagging at this moment.

Why tagging?

In his book Gene Smith gives five reasons why people want to participate in tagging activities:

Managing personal information

A typical example of this kind of tagging can be seen on image sites like *http://picasa.google.com* or *http://www.flickr.com*. The original purpose of these sites was to give people a place to store their photos in a digital album.

Similar to what they used to in a paper album, they could add some keywords or comments to their digital photos too.

Social bookmarking

First of all social bookmarking serves a personal problem. Everybody who stores bookmarks on a PC quickly runs into trouble with them: they are not accessible from another PC or they get lost when something goes wrong with the PC or with the browser. If you store your bookmarks on a bookmark site like *http://www.delicious.com, http://connotea.org, http://www.citeulike.org* or many others; you can access them at any time from any PC with an Internet connection. These sites also have the advantage that you can organize your bookmarks and add keywords/tags to them in order to find them in an easy way when you need them. Because of the fact that these collections of bookmarks are also available to others, a kind of social interaction emerges around them. People who are interested in the same subjects can look in your collection and retrieve your bookmarks in order to build their own collections.

Collecting and sharing digital objects

Photo and video sites on the web may have been started as an answer to the need for a place to store one's personal collections, but they soon became a way to interact socially with friends or people who share the same interests. This purpose was very explicitly built into the Facebook site. Creating virtual communities of friends now is the main purpose. Tagging plays an important role in this: everything can be 'tagged'.

Improving e-commerce

E-commerce sites no longer only offer their goods on the web, they also give the opportunity to the buyers to express their meaning about the products that are sold. Everybody who buys something on Amazon or Buzzillions is asked to express his or her evaluation about the product and everyone who booked a hotel room on *http://www.latebooking.com* can convey his or her experiences with it on the site.

Other reasons

Tagging now has become very successful and a broad range of applications can be found, e.g.

- Museums find in it a way to index collections of old photographs. By putting them on the web with the explicit request to the public to tag them, they hope to learn something about their content.

- Libraries ask their public to tag the books in their catalogues, not that they do not know what their books are about, but they find it a good way to get the public more involved in the activities of the library.

- Until a few months ago, Google asked its public to label its images by means of a 'game with a purpose', the 'imagelabeler'.[1] The game presented an image to two players who could tag them. When the tags coincided the player got a point, but Google got the assurance that this tag probably was accurate for the presented image.

More reasons for tagging may be found, but after reviewing the literature on this subject, Isabella Peters comes to a sobering conclusion: 'So users tag for different reasons' [3: 189]. The most surprising aspect of tagging is that it is so successful.

Apparently many people feel the need to express and share their opinions, anonymously or not, about whatever they see on the web.

Advantages and disadvantages of tagging

Some of the advantages of tagging are:

- Many people just find pleasure or satisfaction in tagging. They spend a lot of their (or their employer's) time on social sites where they comment on what they like or dislike.

- It is a modern form of social interaction. This is very explicit on Facebook and other friendship sites. People not only have real friends but many also have virtual friends they only meet on Facebook.

- Tagging is flexible. Controlled vocabularies mainly express the 'aboutness' of something; tagging makes it possible to articulate your approval or disapproval, or just to be funny.

- Tags do not put the tagged object into one category. They are not bound by the rules to give the most specific term or to assign only one category, as professional library indexers are. They are close to faceting; many aspects of one object can be expressed.

- Tagging can mobilize an army of anonymous 'indexers' who voluntarily help you to index a vast collection of otherwise untraceable photographs.

But tagging certainly has disadvantages too:

- Tags tend to be chaotic. They are entered in many languages, nobody cares about rules like the ones we know from controlled vocabularies, namely that you should not use verbs or adjectives, that you should care about spelling, etc. Some sites try to limit the possibilities by presenting the most popular tags for a certain object or by suggesting choosing from a list.

- They leave the door open for abuse such as obscene or racist language, hate campaigns, swearing, etc. Most sites take precautions and filter this kind of language out, or ask users to report it, but it is not possible to put a stop to everything in any possible language.

- People do not always take their readers into consideration. Tags can have a very special meaning for someone and at the same time mean nothing for the rest of the world. Tagging is full of cryptic abbreviations.

- Tags do not necessarily tell something about what the object is or what it is about. Tag lists on virtual book catalogues like LibraryThing (*http://www.librarything. com/*) are full of tags like 'tbr' (to be read), 'read', 'unread', 'read and sold', 'on list', 'gift from mother', 'wishlist', 'bedroom', etc. They have no relation to the content or subject of the book at hand.

- International tag site are a cacophony of languages.

Towards a taxonomy of tagging

One of the most complete attempts to create a taxonomy of tagging can be found in an article by Heckner *et al.* from 2008 [4]. The authors based their taxonomy on a publication by Margaret Kipp from 2007 [5]. According to Heckner *et al.* tags can be divided into two main categories:

- Subject related tags: tags which say something about the document itself. Here we can make a further distinction between:

- Resource related tags: e.g. tags that contain the name of the author, the date of publication or the source of the document (e.g. the name of the site where it can be found).
- Content related tags: tags that express the content of the document.

■ Non-subject related tags: tags without a direct relation to the document. They express the user's 'current projects, activities and emotional state'. Here a distinction can be made between:

- Affective tags: they express approval or dislike, e.g. 'cool' or 'boring'.
- Time and task related tags (see below).
- Tag avoidance: dummy tags which originate from the fact that certain sites require the user to enter at least one tag. The user who does not want to do so, enters a nonsense tag, e.g. 'no-tag'.

Time and task related tags can be subdivided into:

■ Action related tags: they express what the user did or is going to do with the document (e.g. 'read', 'toread').

■ Context and workflow related tags, expressing the place of the document in the workflow of the user's project (e.g. 'not used', 'printed', 'uploaded').

The content related tags are comparable with what we usually know as keywords. But here too many different kinds are possible:

■ Tags trying to put a document in a certain class.

■ Tags linking a document to a certain discipline.

■ Tags trying to tell something about the subject of the document.

- Tags describing the methodology used ('evaluation', 'qualitative study').

- Tags recording the format of the document ('thesis', 'review', 'journal article').

- Tags expressing the content in a code ('hb1', 'cs631').

Heckner *et al.* catalogue a special kind of tag, which they call 'label tags', into the category 'context and workflow related tags', but it would probably make more sense to see these tags as a kind of classification code and thus as 'content related tags'. They make a distinction between three kinds of label tags:

- Exclusive labels: labels only used by one person (e.g. 'Trs' or '938').

- Shared labels: labels used by more than one person. A typical example is a tag like 'A2' used by students to indicate that the document at hand is related to a course at a certain university or college with code 'A2'.

- Special cases: they found one user with a very exclusive tagging system (with tags like 'data::sequence' or 'data::gen perturbation'). These tags could also be called exclusive labels.

This might be a very good starting point for a fully developed taxonomy of tagging, although some of the categories cannot be clearly separated from each other. Heckner *et al.* conducted their research on *Connotea.org*, a site where bookmarks about scientific literature are stored and tagged. Tagging on other kinds of sites will give a slightly different view. If we look at LibraryThing we can easily find other kinds of tags:

- Administrative tags, expressing e.g. where the user got the book from or where it is now ('Christmas present', 'lent to Frank').

- Tags which express the location of the book: 'bedroom', 'public library'). They can also contain a kind of shelf numbers: 'book 5'.

- Tags contained cataloguing details: '2nd edition', 'hardcover'.

In her book, Isabella Peters gives an overview of many other attempts to build taxonomies of tagging. She comes to the conclusion that we are not yet at the point where a consensus about this subject can be reached [3]. Also, studies about the value of tagging for information retrieval show very different results. Some of them find that retrieval making use of tagging is as efficient as searching by controlled vocabularies, or by means of a search engine like Google [6].

Tagging in the book and library world

At this moment three kinds of tagging in relation to books are popular.

Tagging in virtual library catalogues

At sites like *http://www.librarything.com* or *http://www. goodreads.com* readers can build their own virtual library catalogues. They catalogue the books they have read or that are on their wish list. The tagging system allows them to make all sorts of comments on these books. Some small libraries make use of these sites to build their catalogues and other libraries try to promote their collections by being active on book sites.

Although virtual library catalogues can also allow more 'professional' instruments for indexing, e.g. controlled vocabularies or classifications, the most popular instrument undoubtedly is tagging.

Tagging in book vendor sites

Book vendors encourage buyers to express their opinion about the books they bought. They may also allow buyers to post a complete essay on a book, as well as comments on earlier posted reviews. At Amazon the books from the Harry Potter series may have as many as 4000 reviews and some of these have got 50 or more comments. This practice is not different from the vendor sites where shoes or electronics are tagged.

Tagging in library catalogues

For a few years now many librarians have wanted to join the Web 2.0 hype, and one of the ways to do this is to open library catalogues to tagging. Some catalogues retrieve tags from LibraryThing, others only display the tags directly entered by their own patrons, and others still mix both. This does not mean that the libraries replace their traditional instruments, controlled vocabularies and classifications, by tagging; it is just one more indexing method. The main purpose is not to index the collection by means of tagging, but to have some interaction with the public. Obviously this appeals to the curiosity of (a part of) their public who wants to know what other readers think of the book they want to read.

But the question could be asked whether tagging could replace traditional indexing or not. If this question is answered in a positive way, we could save the money now needed to index the collections by experts. Heyman and

Garcia-Molina conducted a study at Stanford University in 2008 in order to compare tagging af LibraryThing and GoodReads to traditional library instruments as Library of Congress Subject Heading, Dewey Decimal Classification and Library of Congress Classification [7]. Their conclusions were as follows:

- Most tags in both social cataloguing sites were objective and content-based, or in other words, tags do say something about the books.
- Tags divide documents into classes that are similar to those of traditional classifications.
- More than 50 per cent of the top tags are equivalent to terms from controlled vocabularies.
- Tags result in a high recall for popular subjects and a low one for more specialized subjects.
- Tagging does not care for synonyms. Controlled vocabularies have developed instruments to deal with synonyms and nuances between terms.
- The top 500 tags at LibraryThing and GoodReads overlap for 50 per cent.
- Equal documents are indexed in a similar way on both sites; the differences are located in the less popular tags.

A similar study by Rolla in 2009 [8] showed that 75 per cent of the (content-related) tags express the same concept as the LCSH, although some differences may be noted:

- Tags tend to be broad, general, as opposed to specific. Maybe tags are to be compared with classification classes instead of terms from controlled vocabularies.
- Tags sometimes are more specific than controlled terms; they sometimes refer to parts of a book, whereas libraries usually stick to global indexing.

- Usually more tags are attached to a book description than controlled terms. Tagging is not bound by a rule that e.g. only three terms are allowed, as is often the case in libraries.

Normally these kinds of studies come to the conclusion that both tagging and professional indexing have their merits; they are complementary. One of the recommendations in the 2008 report by the Library of Congress Working Group on the Future of Bibliographic Control [9] was to 'develop library systems that can accept user input and other non-library data without interfering with the integrity of library-created data'. This also illustrated the complementary nature of of both systems.

The Open Shelves Classification project is an attempt to get more order in what some see as the chaos on LibraryThing. A group of mostly librarians wants to create a new classification as an instrument for LibraryThing collections. It should become 'a free, "humble", modern, open-source, crowd-sourced replacement for the Dewey Decimal System'.[2] Up until now not much of this has been realized. The activities pretty much stopped after the beginning of 2009.

The question could be asked whether librarians are the right people to create such an instrument. They still rely heavily on classifications that were created in the nineteenth century. They struggle with basic problems attached to them: cultural bias, user unfriendliness, the phenomenon of 'distributed relatives', etc. Recent attempts to find alternatives have not always resulted in the creation of new and better ones; in the USA some libraries now just apply a classification which was built for the bookselling trade, the Book Industry Standards and Communication Classification (BISAC).

User tags and author keywords

Most studies evaluate either tagging or author keywords. Both have more than one aspect in common:

- Both rely mainly on uncontrolled terms, although precautions may have been taken to put some constraint on the freedom of the authors by means of suggestion lists or by limiting the number of terms that can be added etc.

- In both cases the key question, often not explicitly pronounced, is whether they can replace professional indexing or not. If so, a lot of money can be saved. But if we are going to rely on non-professional indexing we should know how to deal with the excesses and the abuse attempts.

- In the library world neither method is yet replacing professional indexing; they are just two of many ways to index a document. Author keywords are found in bibliographic databases next to thesaurus terms, etc. and patron tags appear in our library catalogues next to subject headings and classification terms.

Heckner *et al.* [10] try to compare author keywords with tagging. They only reach a very general conclusion and an attempt to explain the difference between both kinds:

> In general, taggers tend to introduce less and simpler concepts avoiding very specific terms. Although we do not have explicit evidence for this, an explanation might be that authors try to be as specific about the contents of their paper as possible (differentiation strategy with respect to a possibly huge amount of literature in the same field), while taggers try to classify the documents read by them with respect to more general categories [10].

How tags are displayed

Tag clouds

Tag clouds are very popular because they look nice on the screen (Figure 9.1). The size of the characters of each tag corresponds to its importance – at least in principle. It is not possible to show the difference between a tag that was used once, another tag that appears 7000 times and everything in between. Tag cloud builders use tricks to limit the size of the tags. They build classes, e.g. tags that appear less than 100 times get size 1, tags that appear between 100 and 500 times get size 2, etc. There is usually no linear relation between the size and the popularity: at most we can see that one tag is more popular than another. Normally tags are

Figure 9.1   Example of a tag cloud at LibraryThing

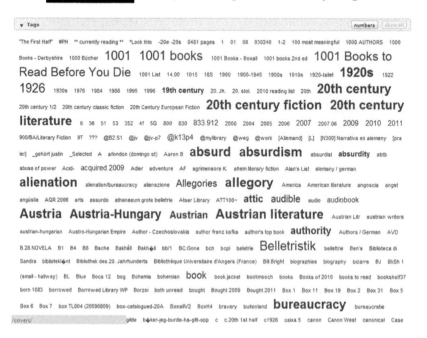

displayed alphabetically, although some experiments have been conducted in order to cluster the tags in a cloud according to their semantic relations [11].

Lists

Sites can display lists of the most used tags. On LibraryThing one can find lists of the top tags, the top long tags, etc. Delicious (*http://www.delicious.com*) produces lists based on clustering of tags that co-appear (Figure 9.2). This also offers to limit the search by clicking on a tag, from the list the user builds a relation with his first tag.

Conclusions

Tagging is here to stay – at least as long as Web 2.0 is going to be popular. We will see that it will grow and mature.

Figure 9.2 **Example of a tag list at Delicious**

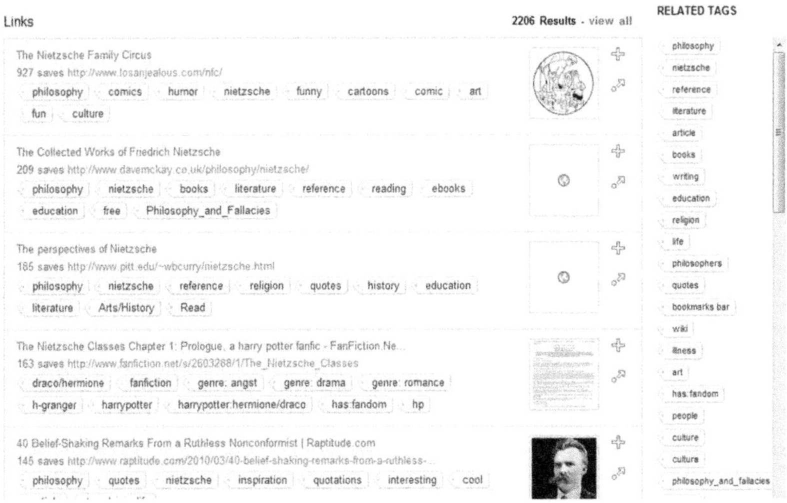

Research will be done in order to find ways to get more out of the immense amount of tags on popular sites, as well as the value for retrieval, which will be subject to more studies. Meanwhile tagging is a complementary indexing tool which can be just one of many, as is the case in our library catalogues, or it can be a good alternative, as is the case in tagging projects where the public is asked to index a collection of photographs that otherwise could not be indexed.

Undoubtedly tagging will play an important part in the Semantic Web. The developers of the Semantic Web understand that tagging has an enormous semantic potential and, as they are not exclusive in their quest for suitable vocabularies, they try to tap the richness of tags as well as the expertise that lies in traditional instruments like thesauri or classifications.

Notes

1. Previously at: *http://images.google.com/imagelabeler*. Google ceased this facility in 2011; the reason why it did so is not known.
2. For more information on the Open Shelves Classification project, see *http://www.librarything.com/wiki/index.php/Open _Shelves_Classification*

References

[1] Morrison, P.J. (2007), 'Why are they tagging, and why do we want them to?', *Bulletin of the ASIST*, 34, 1: 12.

[2] Smith, G. (2008), *Tagging: People-Powered Metadata for the Social Web*. Berkeley, CA: New Riders,

[3] Peters, I. (2009), *Folksonomies: Indexing and Retrieval in Web 2.0*. Berlin: De Gruyter-Saur.

[4] Heckner, M., Mühlbacher, S. and Wolff, C. (2008), 'Tagging tagging: analysing user keywords in scientific bibliography management systems', *Journal of Digital Information*; 2. Available from: *http://journals.tdl.org/jod/article/view/246/208*

[5] Kipp, M.E.I. (2007), '@toread and cool: tagging for time, task and emotion', Proceedings of the 8th Information Architecture Summit, Las Vegas, Nevada, March 22–26, 2007. Available from: *http://eprints.rclis.org/17669/1/mkipp-sigcrposter-ASSIST2006.pdf*

[6] Morrison, P.J. (2008), 'Tagging and searching: search retrieval effectiveness of folksonomies on the World Wide Web', *Information Processing and Management*, 44: 1562–79.

[7] Heyman, P. and Garcia-Molina, H. (2008), 'Can tagging organize human knowledge?' InfoLab Technical report to Stanford University. Available from: *http://ilpubs.stanford.edu:8090/878/1/ltoc.pdf*

[8] Rolla, P.J. (2009), 'User tags versus subject headings: can user-supplied data improve subject access to library collections?', *Library Resources & Technical Services*, 53: 174–84.

[9] Library of Congress (2008), 'On the record: report of the Library of Congress Working Group on the Future of Bibliographic Control', p. 2. Available from: *http://www.loc.gov/bibliographic-future/news/lcwg-ontherecord-jan08-final.pdf*

[10] Heckner, M., Mühlbacher, S. and Wolff, C. (2008), 'Tagging tagging: analysing user keywords in scientific bibliography management systems', *Journal of Digital Information*, p. 2. Available from: *http://journals.tdl.org/jod/article/view/246/208*

[11] Wartena, C. (2010), 'Tagvarianten semantisch getemd', *Informatie Professional*, 3: 20–3 (in Dutch).

10

Topic Maps

Abstract: Topic Maps can be compared to indexes at the back of a book: in an index a subject term (topic) refers to a certain page (occurrence) and relations between terms are defined (associations). Different standards, tools and examples regarding Topic Maps can be found on the web. The champions of Topic Maps may present it as an alternative for traditional indexing and as a remedy to the chaos they believe to be inherent to automatic indexing. They also regard it as the next logical step in the evolution of the web, but the question can be asked whether Topic Maps are going to be more successful than or integrated into the Semantic Web instruments.

Key words: Topic Maps, HyTime, XTM, Omnigator, TAO model.

Introduction

Librarians generally have a lot of sympathy for Topic Maps because they resemble the tools they know very well: indexes in books and controlled vocabularies. Topic Maps promoters see Topic Maps as a third revolution in the history of the World Wide Web:

- 1991: first revolution: the creation of the web.
- 1997: second revolution: the creation of XML.
- 2003: third revolution: Topic Maps.

Publications about Topic Maps always begin with a comparison between Topic Maps and book indexing. Book indexes are alphabetical lists of all the subjects (topics) that are discussed in the book, and the pages on which these subjects can be found. But indexes don't just use words from the text; all terms in an index must at least apply to these criteria:

- Only meaningful words are selected.

- Stop words are disregarded.

- The words from the text are transformed into their corresponding index term, which may e.g. mean that nouns are always in the plural.

In other words: making book indexes implies a lot of controlling, whereas full text indexing is not necessarily controlled. Topic Maps are presented as an alternative to full text indexing: they are supposed to be the opposite of what traditionally is regarded as the major disadvantages of full text indexing:

- Relevant and irrelevant words are treated equally.

- No choice is made between synonyms.

- There is no way to discriminate between homonyms.

As was stipulated in Chapters 2 and 3, this is a common prejudice against full text indexing which the champions of Topic Maps sometimes take for granted. All in all, Topic Maps should offer the best of three worlds:

- The world of book indexing.

- Traditional library indexing techniques (subject headings and thesauri).

- Knowledge management (especially the way KM uses graphical representations of knowledge processes).

Topic Maps are defined in an ISO/IEC standard, i.e. ISO/IEC 13250, of which versions and substandards can be found here and there on the web, which is quite unusual for ISO standards.[1] These documents may be rather technical; a better way to learn about Topic Maps is probably to read one of these websites: *http://www.topicmaps.org* or *http://www.ontopedia.net*.

The TAO model of Topic Maps

Topic Maps[2] are built around three important concepts: topics, associations and occurrences between topics. As a happy coincidence these three basic words form the acronym TAO, which in Taoism means 'the way'.

Topics

Everything can be a topic; this roughly resembles what we spontaneously would call 'subjects'. The topics can be categorized in types, which, again, is similar to what is standard practice in book indexing: an index for names of persons, geographical names, art works, etc.

Occurrences

An occurrence is an object that corresponds with a topic. This can be a work of art, a website, a book, a video, a picture etc. In Topic Maps theory it is emphasized that these objects are external to topics: occurrences and topics have a relation to each other, whereas keywords drawn from a text through automatic full text indexing are parts of these texts.

Associations

Associations express the relation between two or more topics, e.g.

'Hamlet' *was written by* William Shakespeare.

Paris *is the capital* of France.

A carburettor *is a part* of a motor vehicle engine.

Julius Caesar *conquered* Gaul.

Topics can have more than one kind of association:

Nietzsche is one of the most important nineteenth-century philosophers.

Nietzsche was a source of inspiration for Nazism.

Nietzsche wrote *Also sprach Zarathustra*.

Nietzsche is a precursor to existentialism.

Nietzsche was a friend of Paul Rey and Lou Salomé.

A topic is not necessarily connected to an occurrence and every relation can, in turn, be a topic: 'being an inspiration source', 'being a friend', etc. To this extent topics are different from book indexes:

- A term in a book index refers always to a certain part of the text.
- Some terms in book indexes are related ('See:' and 'See also:'), but this is not necessarily so; in Topic Maps, relations between topics are essential.

The technical side of Topic Maps

The concept of Topic Maps may be quite understandable, as it is in concept very similar to the well-known practices of building book indexes or indexing a book collection with a thesaurus, which have both been done manually for a very long time by publishers and librarians. If we want to build computer applications for Topic Maps, we need to be much more technical. A few code systems for Topic Maps were developed:

- HyTime, a markup language built on SGML: HyTime dates from the pre-XML years, i.e. the beginning of the 1990s.
- XTM, i.e. the XML way to encode Topic Maps.

Here is an example of a Topic Map in XTM. In human language this would read 'When in New York, visit the Brooklyn Bridge':[3]

```
<topic id='t1'>
<baseName><baseNameString>New    York</baseNameString>
   </baseName>
</topic>

<topic id='b298'>
<baseName><baseNameString>Brooklyn    Bridge</baseName
   String>
</baseName></topic>

<association>
<member>
<roleSpec><topicRef xlink:href='#when-in'/></roleSpec>
<topicRef xlink:href='#t1'/></member>
<member>
<roleSpec><topicRef xlink:href= 'visit'/></roleSpec>
<topicRef xlink:href= 'b298'/></member>
</association>
```

Examples of Topic Maps

Like taxonomy builders, Topic Map creators get their inspiration from very different sources:

- ontologies;

- taxonomies, classifications, thesauri;

- metadata schemes;

- indexes, glossaries.

The website *http://www.ontopia.net/omnigator/models/index.jsp* offers some examples of Topic Maps and lets you navigate through their relations (Figure 10.1). It also offers a way of representing the Topic Maps graphically (Figure 10.2).

Figure 10.1   Omnigator

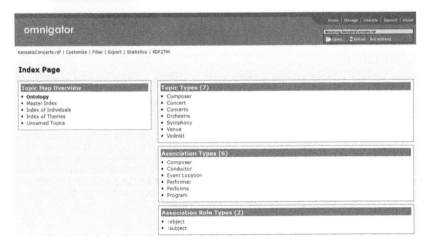

Figure 10.2 Graphical display of a Topic Map in Omnigator

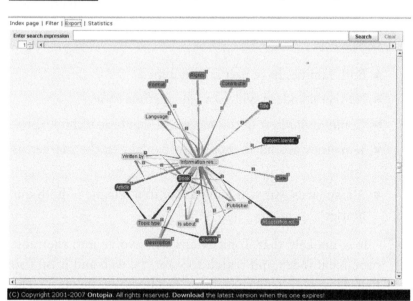

Are Topic Maps the future of indexing?

Topic Maps were once called 'the GPS of the information universe' [1], and in the introduction to this chapter we mentioned that librarians have sympathy towards them, but this doesn't mean that a lot of effort has been invested in creating Topic Maps. In fact Topic Maps is just one of many indexing tools that were developed almost simultaneously:

- taxonomies and ontologies
- Topic Maps
- the Semantic Web tools.

Some rivalry exists between the champions of different systems, but there are also a lot of attempts to recover rivals into one's own system. On a website Steve Pepper, Chief Strategy Officer of Ontopia, lists the differences between

Topic Maps and RDF, a basic tool for the Semantic Web (see Chapter 12), but he highlights the synergies between the two systems and emphasizes the dangers of letting the rivalry persist [2]:

- Both families have user communities.

- Neither standard will go away anytime soon.

- Common interest in the success of semantic technologies.

- Semantics are hard enough to explain to the market as it is.

- A standards war will indeed lead to a 'Plague o' both our houses'.

It is unlikely that Topic Maps will evolve into the most prominent index and search tool for the web and it isn't so that they will replace subject headings or thesauri. The concept behind Topic Maps is as good as those behind other modern indexing tools, but they have probably stood on their own for too long.

Notes

1. See e.g. *http://www.itscj.ipsj.or.jp/sc34/open/1045.htm*
2. A very comprehensive introduction to the TAO of Topic Maps can be found at: *http://www.ontopia.net/topicmaps/materials/tao.html*
3. This example is taken from: *http://www.infoloom.com/xtmg_codeexamples.htm*

References

[1] Wittenbrink, H. (2000), 'The "GPS of the information universe": Topic Maps in an encyclopaedic online

information platform', web article. Available from *http://www.infoloom.com/gcaconfs/WEB/paris2000/S11-04.HTM*

[2] Pepper, S. (2005), 'A plague o' both our houses?', web article. Available from: *http://www.w3.org/2005/Talks/03-lt-pepper/plague.html*

11

Indexing the web

Abstract: Some libraries catalogue websites as if they were books. Other initiatives to manually index (part) of the web are web directories and web pages. Web directories offer a structured way to retrieve websites. Startpages, a typically Dutch phenomenon, list all their links in one page. Social bookmarks too are a kind of manual web indexing: many people save relevant links on a bookmark site and in doing so help to build a manual index. The most important role is played by the automatic web indexing mechanisms search engines use. Google has overcome the ranking problem all search engines face. The PageRank mechanism sorts the retrieved web pages according to the links they receive from other sites. Some search engines specialize in indexing the 'deep web', the information hidden in databases, but they still manage to index only part of it.

Key words: web indexing, web directories, startpages, social bookmarks, PageRank, deep web.

Is it possible to index the web?

The Internet contains all kinds of information. This information may be in different formats: HTML files, PDF documents, Power Point presentations, images in JPEG or GIF format, etc., moving images, executable programmes, compressed files, etc. Some of them are freely accessible, others are hidden behind passwords. Even if we look at a simple HTML page this does not mean we see all of it: part of it remains invisible as the codes or commands behind it that generate the page.

Appearances are deceptive: the pages we find on the web may not exist as such. They may be constructed on the spot from information stored in databases each time we click on a button, and a click by a different searcher can format the same information in a different way and produce a different web page. These pages are not static, but dynamic.

The naïve web searcher, using Google or another popular search engine, gets the impression that everything he finds is some kind of static page that exists, on the web, somewhere. He may be irritated when he tries to open a page that no longer exists or does not contain the information it should have according to the index of the search engine. Baeza-Yates and Ribeiro-Neto compared this to the images we have of the stars: we think that every dot of light we see in the sky is in fact a star that is shining now, whereas many of them were extinguished billions of years ago [1].

All this can only discourage us to try and index the web. But does it really? From the early 1990s, when the Internet was finally made available to non-academic users, libraries have tried to catalogue interesting websites in their catalogues, and some still do. Some library catalogues contain descriptions of web pages as if they were paper documents. They are catalogued according to the same rules that are used to catalogue books. The Flemish central catalogue for the public libraries contains about 7600 websites. Knowing that they are only a very small part of the web, the public libraries still find it necessary to catalogue them.

Although automatic indexing by search engines, like Google, Altavista, Yahoo!, LookSmart and many others, is extremely successful, thousands of people find it necessary to create manual web indexes, or at least to contribute to one.

Manual web indexes

All kinds of indexes can be found, ranging from small ones, i.e. a few links on a page, to universal web directories, e.g. *http://www.dmoz.org,* which has more than four and a half million links. Web indexes can be categorized according to different sorts of criteria:

- by subject, e.g. environmental information: *http://www. webdirectory.com;*
- by geographical region or country, e.g. for New Zealand: *http://webdirectory.natlib.govt.nz/index.htm;*
- by type of information, e.g. scientific information: *http:// www.sciencedirectory.info;*
- by author, e.g. the Librarians' Internet Index: *http://lii.org;*
- etc.

On a formal basis, there are two (main) kinds of manual index:

Web directories

Web directories have a home page with only a limited number of subjects. In fact these are the main classes of a classification. Clicking on one of the classes will lead to one or more subclasses, which themselves will have more subclasses, etc.: the classes have a hierarchical order. If you want to find bicycle shops in England on the DMOZ web directory

| Figure 11.1 | Search results in DMOZ |

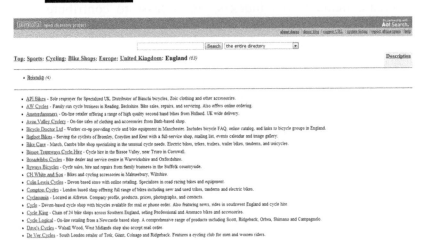

(*http://www.dmoz.org*; see also Figure 11.1), you will have to descend along these steps of the hierarchical ladder:

Sports

    Cycling

        Bike Shops

            Europe

                United Kingdom

                England

DMOZ is the largest web directory in the world and was adopted for some years by Google as its 'Google Directory'. More than 90 000 volunteer editors take part in it. These editors, who may fulfil one of seven different tasks, are all idealists working for free.[1] DMOZ describes them as people 'who still believe that the web should be free and accessible to all, without bias and unnecessary noise'.

From the end of the nineteenth century, and especially in the first half of the twentieth century, classification theory was developed by library and information scientists. This theory forms the basis of our library classifications, e.g. the Universal Decimal Classification, the Dewey Decimal Classification, etc. The rules are rather strict, because their purpose is to create order in knowledge and sciences and because classifications are also used to shelve library books: each book must have a fixed and predictable location in the library. The way subject categories are ordered in a web directory seems much less rigorous. On the main page of DMOZ (Figure 11.2) we find 'Games' or 'Sports' at the same level as 'Recreation', whereas one would think that games and sports are both a kind of recreation.

Figure 11.2 Main page of DMOZ

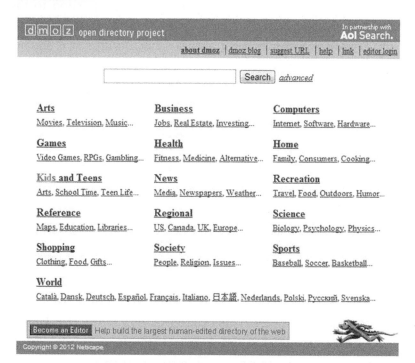

Most directories follow a different kind of logic than library classifications: not strict scientific categorization, but user-friendliness is important. A searcher who starts at one point must find the same information as one who chooses a slightly different access point. Therefore 'Recreation' and 'Sports' are also part of 'Recreation' in DMOZ. This kind of circular classification may be an unforgivable sin for students of library classifications, but it makes sense in web directories. This does not mean that there are no rules behind web directories. Normally web directories should at least adhere to these rules:[2]

- The classification should be transparent and allow the user to see at each step where he started from and how he can continue.

- The number of subclasses must be in proportion to the number of links. It is not good practice if a click on a subclass produces a list of thousands of links. It is equally wrong to force the user to choose more than ten subclasses in order to find only one or a few links.

- The classification must correspond to the standard subdivision in sciences, trades, etc. Those categories are relatively fixed, but it is difficult to find acceptable subdivisions for trivial subject areas like 'Home', 'Children', 'Leisure', etc.

Although library classifications are generally not used to build web directories, some can be found on the web. The best known – and one of the oldest – probably is *http://www.bubl.ac.uk* (formerly known as the Bulletin Board for Libraries) of the Centre for Digital Library Research at Strathclyde University in Glasgow, based on the Dewey Digital Classification (see Figure 11.3). It still exists, but it has not beem updated since 2011.

Figure 11.3   The BUBL web directory

BUBL LINK Catalogue of Internet Resources

The BUBL service is no longer being updated (April 2011)

Dewey | Search | Subject Menus | Countries | Types | BUBL UK | BUBL Archive

Selected Internet resources covering all academic subject areas

A | B | C | D | E | F | G | H | I | J | K | L | M | N | O | P | Q | R | S | T | U | V | W | X | Y | Z

000 Generalities
Includes: computing, Internet, libraries, information science

100 Philosophy and psychology
Includes: ethics, paranormal phenomena

200 Religion
Includes: bibles, religions of the world

300 Social sciences
Includes: sociology, politics, economics, law, education

400 Language
Includes: linguistics, language learning, specific languages

500 Science and mathematics
Includes: physics, chemistry, earth sciences, biology, zoology

600 Technology
Includes: medicine, engineering, agriculture, management

700 The arts
Includes: art, planning, architecture, music, sport

800 Literature and rhetoric
Includes: literature of specific languages

900 Geography and history
Includes: travel, genealogy, archaeology

[Search]

E-LIS | CDLR Projects | Contacts and Credits

BUBL uses the Dewey Decimal Classification system as the primary organisation structure for its catalogue of Internet resources.
The Dewey Decimal Classification is (c) 1996-2007 OCLC Online Computer Library Center. Used with Permission.

'Startpages'

An interesting phenomenon in the world of web indexes are 'startpages'. They are very successful in the Netherlands, and the English entries that can be found are mostly English versions of Dutch startpages. Startpages have a flatter structure than web directories; the main page contains links to a selection of web pages, ordered by subject. Any kind of layout can be applied to a startpage, but many of them have a very typical layout, as in Figure 11.4. If a subject is extensive, the startpage may link to a new one, covering only that subject. This is called a 'daughter'. The Dutch *http:// www.startpagina.nl* has almost 6000 daughters, some of which are quite amusing:

- *snurken.startpagina.nl*: about snoring;
- *sokken.startpagina.nl*: about socks;
- *langemensen.startpagina.nl*: about tall people;
- *garagedeuren.startpagina.nl*: about garage doors;

Figure 11.4   A 'startpage' at *http://www.mystart.co.uk*

News & Weather [X]
BBC News
BBC World
CNN Europe
Recentnews.co.uk
ITN News
Info. clearing house
newspapers & magazines
The Daily Mirror
The Guardian
The Independent
The Telegraph
This is London
more newspapers & magazines
.. Mediauk.com▶
weather
BBC weather
ITV weather
The Met Office
Weatheronline.co.uk

Blogs [X]
BBC blog network
Bloglines.com
Blogger.com
Britblog
Google blog search
Spyblog

Sport [X]
BBC Sport
Eurosport
Rivals.net
Sky Sports
Sportal UK
Sporting Life
Sportsweb
sport pick
boxing Boxercise
boxing Secondsout.com
cricket Cricinfo.com

Search UK [X]
UK search directories
@UK
Altavista
Ask Jeeves
UK directory
UK Plus
Yahoo UK and Ireland
telephone directories
The Phone Book (BT)
Yell.com
post & postal codes
Royal Mail
people search
1901censusonline.com
1911census.co.uk
Family Records Gov. UK
Findmypast.com
Friends Reunited
Scotlands people
maps
Streetmap.co.uk
Multimap
Old-maps.co.uk
Npemap.org.uk
Railwaysarchive.co.uk

Travel UK [X]
Airport Timetables
Airtraffic.eu
Bettertransport.org.uk
Cheapflights
Foreign Office Travel Advice
Globalbagtag
National Rail Enquiries
Highway Agency
Realholidayreports.com
Thetrams.co.uk
Transportdirect.info
Traveline.org.uk
more TRAVEL UK▶

Personal Settings [X]
your bookmarks & personal stuff!
Change Your Bookmarks
Address book
Calculator
Date reminder
Memo Block

Desktop Helpers [X]
dates & times
Calendar
Earthcalendar.net
Timeanddate.com
World time
money & conversions
XE.com
Convert-me.com
language
Onelook.com
Systransoft.com
Thesaurus.com
useful references
Allexperts.com
ehow.com
Encyclopedia.com
Expertvillage.com
Lifehacker.com
Reference.com
Weeno.com
Whichbook.net

E-Mail / E-Cards [X]
e-mail
Gmail
Hotmail
Latinmail
Spamcop.net
Twigger.com
Yahoo
e-cards
Bluemountain.com
Hallmark.co.uk

- *geluk.startpagina.nl*: about happiness;
- etc.

The indexing technique behind it is the same as with web directories: every link to a website has to be selected manually. But there are essential differences between the two:

- Web directories are tree structures: you have to climb down the tree in order to find what you are looking for. Startpages are flat: every link is directly on the main page.

- Web directories normally give some kind of abstract of the sites they link to. Startpages just offer the links.

Bookmark sites

Bookmark sites are kinds of folksonomies: people save digital information and add tags to it. As well as other kinds of folksonomies, e.g. photo sites like Flickr, video sites, etc., they are not intended to be a way of indexing; they serve other purposes. People save web links on the Internet when they want to archive them for personal use or when they want to share them with everyone who may have the same interests. The keywords they add are meant to make it easier for themselves to retrieve what they saved, but they can also be used as search terms by someone who is searching for information. These are some (famous) examples of bookmark sites:

http://del.icio.us

On *http://del.icio.us* everyone can save their bookmarks. It may be safer than saving them on your own PC, where they will probably disappear if some serious software problem occurs. This may be the primary purpose of using del.icio.us. When you save a bookmark, you can add one or more 'tags' to it. The website gives this explanation of 'tags': 'Tags are one-word descriptors that you can assign to your bookmarks on del.icio.us to help you organize and remember them. Tags are a little bit like keywords, but they're chosen by you, and they do not form a hierarchy. You can assign as many tags to a bookmark as you like and rename or delete the tags later.'

A website about cats (*http://www.stuffonmycat.com/*), which was saved by almost 2000 people, gets these tags: 'cats', 'humour', 'funny', 'blog', 'photos', 'fun', 'animals', 'photography', 'cat', 'cute', 'blogs', 'photo', 'stuff', 'weird', 'pictures', 'images', 'pets', 'cool', 'daily', 'gallery', 'awesome', 'comedy', 'web', 'silly'. This would make any librarian's hair stand on end, but apparently people (the folk!) think of their favourite website on cats as 'that weird one' or 'my stuff' or my 'cool' bookmark, etc.

http://connotea.org

Connotea is meant for scientists and researchers who want to save references of scientific literature. In doing so, they can share them with others who might be interested in the same subject. Connotea offers the possibility to add 'keywords for easy retrieval'. The website explains this option as follows (*http://connotea.org*):

> When you save a reference to Connotea, you add keywords (or 'tags') to the reference to help you find it again. You can choose any tags you like, and each reference can have as many tags as you like, so you will never have to decide between different categories or navigate complex folder structures.

In other words: anything goes. Of course, this results in all kinds of personal keywords, in many languages.

These are only a few prototypes of bookmark sites; many others may be found. And many ways to use and re-use manual web indexing may be found too. We already referred to what Google did with DMOZ. Another example is the way websites are indexed in the central catalogue of the Flemish public libraries in Belgium. This catalogue (*http://*

zoeken.bibliotheek.be) contains about 7600 descriptions of web pages, which also build the content of the web directory of the same public libraries (*http://webwijzer.bibliotheek.be*). This example shows that even libraries in a small community with limited resources still find it necessary to invest in manual web indexing, notwithstanding the fact that a vast international web directory like DMOZ is also available in other languages than English (DMOZ can be searched in Dutch, the official language in Flanders).

So, what are the advantages of manual web indexing?

Evaluation of manual web indexing

Manual web indexing has some advantages:

- Information found in manual indexes may be of better quality than the information search engines provide because of the fact that someone went through the trouble of evaluating it and adding it to a list.
- The information usually is clearly classified and presented.
- Often a short description or some sort of tagging of the website is provided.
- Mostly these indexes allow browsing; the user does not have to guess search terms.

But manual indexes may also have some disadvantages:

- There can be low consistency in the tree structures: lots of overlap, a discrepancy between the number of notes in the structure and the links to be found.
- Although the content is selected by humans and not by some program, it is not always clear on which criteria the selection is done.

- Not all manual indexes provide some kind of description of the documents they index.

- The user may not always find what he is looking for. He will have to use other tools to retrieve the information he needs.

These other tools probably will be provided by a search engine.

Web indexing by search engines

Since the mid 1990s, search engines have been the most popular way to find information on the Internet. Before the birth of search engines other tools – mostly very limited in their scope – were used to search the Internet, e.g. gophers, a kind of web directory. The naïve web user has the impression that everything on the Internet can be found by using a search engine, especially Google, the apparent 'number one' among search engines. In fact, this is not the case. Google says that it indexes 8 billion web pages, but the web contains many more pages, at least double that amount. Moreover, an enormous amount of information is stored in the 'deep web', the web of databases. Normally it can only be found if you use the search interface the database offers – and even then accessing the information may be exclusively limited to clients who pay for it.

A database vendor like EbscoHost (*http://www.ebscohost.com/*) offers several hundreds of databases, all containing thousands (and in some of them more than one million) of references and full text articles. Only a few of Ebsco's databases are searchable without subscription. In specialized literature, very different estimates about the scale of the 'deep' or 'hidden web' can be found: it is believed to be 20, 30, 50, times the size of the visible web. In fact, nobody knows, but one thing is certain: it must be enormous.

Sometimes librarians still pretend that the information they offer is of better quality than what one can find by means of search engines – although they probably are active Google users themselves. Some arguments often heard against search engines are:

- Any search leads to a list of thousands of references presented without any evaluation.
- The web is full of commercial ads, pornography and other worthless information.
- Search engines can be manipulated so that the information that is most prominently presented (at the top of the list) might not be the most relevant.

To some extent all of this is true. It is a huge problem to filter out the good bits on the web and provide some ranking in all the possible answers to a search. Google's way of doing this is unique and has proved to be very successful. Before we explain the technique behind Google, let us first have a look at the way search engines work in general.

How search engines work

Search engines have 'spiders', also called 'crawlers', i.e. programs that skim the web to retrieve as many web pages and other documents as possible. Copies of these are stored in a database, which is indexed. Any search by a search engine first goes to that index and the list you see as a result of the search comes from the database, not directly from the web itself. Only if you click on the title of the document will you be connected to the page itself – at least if it still exists. This principle is rather simple, provided that you can program a 'spider' and that you have the necessary software and enough hardware to store and redistribute all the information (it is said that Google uses 10 000 computers . . .). The real challenge lies in the way the information will be ranked. In the 1990s this was not a problem yet: web searchers were happy with each new search engine that gave more answers than the previous one. But by the turn of the century, search engines which showed no or poor ranking fell back or even disappeared.

The whole point of ranking in regard to indexing is that from all the many documents a search engine presents as the result of a query, only those which are highest ranked will be consulted. It does not matter that all documents were indexed equally well and that the search terms are also present in the lowest ranked one; nobody can read the 28 900 000 documents Google finds on the Olympic Games; we can probably never even reach the end of the list. For those documents which are deep down in the list, the situation is equal to not being indexed at all.

Dirk Lewandowski makes a distinction between query-dependent ranking and query-independent ranking by search engines [2]: 'Query-dependent factors are all ranking factors that are specific to a given query, while query-independent factors are attached to the documents, regardless of a given query [2: 142]. As 'query-dependent factors' Lewandowski names:

- *Word document frequency*: the document that contains the search term more than another is ranked higher.

- *Search term distance*: if a search term consists of more than one word the documents in which these words are adjacent to one another are more relevant.

- *Search term order*: the same condition as the previous, but even more strict.

- *Position of the query terms*: documents in which the search term is in the title are probably more relevant.

- *Metatags*: if the search term is in the keyword area of the web page, it probably tells more about its content.

- *Position of the search term within the document*: if the term is at the beginning of the document, the chance that it is important is bigger.

- *Emphasis on terms within the document*: words in bold or italics may be more meaningful than others.

- *Inverted document frequency*: documents with specific terms have a higher value than documents with words that appear in any document.

- *Anchor text*: terms in anchor text added to photos define the subject of that photo.

- *Language*: a document in the language of the searcher may be of more interest to him.

- *Geo targeting*: documents located nearer to the searcher may captivate his attention the most.

The trouble with query-dependent ranking factors is that they are relatively easy to manipulate. If you want your porn site to be found by anyone who is looking for used cars, just add 'used cars' and maybe a lot of names of car makes as keywords to your pages. And if you even want it to be found first, keep on repeating those keywords as many times as possible, of course invisibly. These kinds of tricks to deceive search engines based on query-dependent ranking were becoming common practice in the 1990s and still are. This forced search engines to be very suspicious about some of these techniques and even to disregard them altogether.

Query-independent ranking factors are:

- *Directory hierarchy*: documents placed higher in the structure of the web site may be more important.

- *Number of incoming links*: the more other websites link to a certain document, the more prominent it is in regard to the subject.

- *Click popularity*: if a document is chosen more times in a given list, it has to be better than others which are less or not chosen.

- *Up-to-dateness*: if a document is never updated, the information it contains may be old and of lesser value.

- *Document length*: a longer document can treat the subject better than a short one.

- *File format*: a search engine for scientific information prefers documents in PDF or DOC, others may rank HTML higher.

- *Size of the website*: documents which are part of a large website may be of higher quality than an occasional lonely page.

Query-independent ranking techniques can be questioned too, and especially the emphasis on incoming links is subject to criticism:

- Search engines based on query-independent ranking are biased. They take it for granted that a web page which has more incoming links is better, or that a frequently updated one is better than one which content is stable, etc. In doing so they assume that quality is equal to success or change, etc., which is a very debatable principle.

- Web pages link to other pages for different reasons. In fact, one can even link to another page on the same subject because the content of it is considered to be totally incorrect.

■ Query-independent ranking can also be manipulated, as we will see further on.

The success of Google was mainly based on its unique ranking mechanism in which the number of the incoming links a page gets is the most prominent factor – although Google, like other search engines, uses a combination of query-dependent and query-independent factors.

Google's PageRank

Search engine companies are very secretive about their ranking algorithms, and they have good reasons to be so. Their success depends on it and if they do not want their competitors to copy it, they'd better protect their secrets. In the case of Google the principle of its ranking mechanism, which Google calls its 'PageRank', is well known due to the fact that Google's founders, Lawrence Page and Sergey Brin, published it (in collaboration with others) in a paper back in 1999 when they were still doing research at Stanford University [3].[3]

For Google, every page initially has the same value. Let's say that each page starts with a value of 100. When another page links to this page, (some of) the other page's value is added to this initial value. The source page does not give its value away, but when it links to two other pages only half of its PageRank is added to each one of those pages. In the scheme illustrated in Figure 11.5, page A links to B and C and in doing so it distributes half of its PageRank to each of them, while keeping its initial 100. When C then links to D and E, it now has more PageRank to distribute, as in Figure 11.6.

Figure 11.5 Links between websites

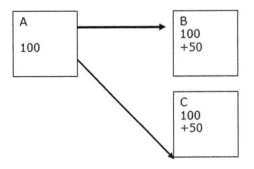

Figure 11.6 More links between websites

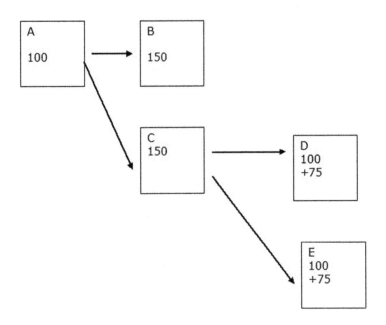

Of course the situation can be far more complex than the one shown:

- A page can link to another one, which itself can link back to the former. In this case the calculating of the PageRank becomes circular (Google has a mechanism to let this go on for some time until it is considered to be enough).

- A page probably is part of a website. Each page in a website can link to other pages in the same site and in doing so the site gives PageRank to its own pages. As a consequence, the PageRank it can distribute to other sites is lower: it is keeping its PageRank inside. If the pages of a site only link to external pages, it is said to be 'leaking' PageRank.

The calculation of the PageRank is not that simple either. The formula may look like this [4]:

$$PR(A) = (1-d) + d(PR(t1)/C(t1) + \ldots + PR(tn)/C(tn)) \quad [11.1]$$

where:

PR(A) is the PageRank of a page;

d is a moderating factor (estimated to be 0.85);

PR(t1) to PR(tn) is the PageRank of pages linking to A;

C(t1) to C(tn) are the number of outgoing links in those pages.

But Google does not just rank pages on a linear scale: it uses a logarithmic one (probably log5 or log6). The consequence of this is that a page needs a multitude of its actual incoming links to get to the next level in the ranking.

Because the PageRank mechanism is in principle well known, attempts are made to manipulate the ranking:

- 'Link farms' are sites of which the only purpose is to link as many times as possible to the clients' web pages in order to raise the PageRank.

- Some authors of websites post a lot of messages with links to their own pages to blogs and discussion lists.

They may have been successful in the beginning, but now Google takes the necessary measures to detect this kind of activity. The punishment for a website that tries to raise its PageRank in this way is that its PageRank is reduced to zero.

This does not mean that nothing is allowed: some measures can be taken to get a better PageRank in a fair way, e.g.

- One can exchange links: ask a webmaster of a site with a similar content to link to your pages and offer to link to his site.
- Building links between your own pages.

Everyone who has a webpage now and then receives spam mail proposing new variations to the link farm trick. I found the following mail in my spam box:

> Hello,
>
> Let's do a 3-way link swap with your website http://[...]. I'll give you two links in exchange for one from you. 3-way linking is a very effective link building strategy. Since you're getting the links from third party websites, they appear totally natural to search engines. Such inbound links help your website rank higher in Google and other search engines. (The name of the website is omitted by the author)

The proposal is to interchange only a few links so that Google does not get suspicious. But it is still a way to deceive the system because there is no relation whatever between the content of my webpage and the pages that are going to link to me. The foundation of the Google PageRank is the supposition that web pages link to other pages because they have something in common or because the authors find it important enough to draw attention to them. Once we just link for the sake of the PageRank, we try to abuse the system.

In 2006 Amy N. Langville and Carl D. Meyer published an entire book on the mathematics behind Google's PageRank [5] based on matrices, vectors and Markov chains. This proves that it is not a simple trick. But linking is not everything according to Google. Some 80 factors, of which only 70 were found in many tests and published in specialized literature or on the web, are used to build the ranking. Google gives some explanation on its website but tries to keep its secrets well hidden at the same time:

> Google uses many factors in ranking. Of these, the PageRank algorithm might be the best known. [. . .] But we use many factors besides PageRank. For example, if a document contains the words 'civil' and 'war' right next to each other, it might be more relevant than a document discussing the Revolutionary War that happens to use the word 'civil' somewhere else on the page. Also, if a page includes the words 'civil war' in its title, that's a hint that it might be more relevant than a document with the title '19th Century American Clothing.' In the same way, if the words 'civil war' appear several times throughout the page, that page is more likely to be about the civil war than if the words only appear once [6].

Is this the whole truth or does Google really use PigeonRank?[4]

What about indexing the 'deep web'?

The 'deep web' causes two problems: one for the indexer, because his webcrawler cannot access the information in it, and one for the searcher, who cannot find information hidden in it using his favourite tool, the search engine.

We all know that the 'deep web' is many times larger than the visible web. But how large is it really? Researchers have published some figures, although they are at best estimations. In a 2007 article, Bin He, Mitesh Patel, Zhen Zhang and Kevin Chen-Chuan Chang [7] calculated that the 'deep web' must contain some 307 000 sites, housing about 450 000 databases. Some search engines specialize in the 'deep web' and even then most of them specialize in a certain aspect of it, e.g. scientific information. Bin He *et al.* found that turbo10.com, a general deep web search engine that existed from 2000 until 2010, indexed only 0.5 per cent of the deep web.[5] Search engines like Google, Yahoo or MSN index only one-third of the information in the 'deep web'. Some of them at least try to index the 'deep web'. Bin *et al.* came to the conclusion that 'the deep web remains largely unexplored and is currently neither well supported nor well understood' [7].

'Open archives' are databases based on protocols which are meant to be as open as possible. Documents stored in open archives can be 'harvested' by other services; the retrieval of the data in it does not exclusively depend on the search interface of its own database. One would expect that those documents can also be reached and indexed by webcrawlers of search engines. Research revealed that Yahoo can find 65 per cent of them, Google 44 per cent and MSN 7 per cent, and that 21 per cent are not indexed by these three search engines at all [8]. In a number of cases the search engines are not to be blamed for this, but the open archives themselves. Some of them contain a file, a 'robots.txt' (well known to webmasters), in which they tell webcrawlers not to follow links on their pages. This attitude, which is contradictory to the philosophy of 'open' archives, is mostly a reaction to the high pressure webcrawlers put upon database software when they try to extract information, which may cause overload on a server.

Not only databases, but also websites based on databases, i.e. 'dynamic websites' pose problems for search engines and their crawlers. These websites are programmed in languages like PHP or ASP, which retrieve information from a database, format it and present it on the web as a 'normal', static HTML page each time the user clicks on one of the links in it. The problem for a webcrawler is that it can find and index the main page of the website but is not able to retrieve the information from the database behind it: it cannot 'click' on the links it finds in the main page.

Webmasters can read this answer to the question 'does Google index dynamic pages?' in Google's 'Webmaster Help Center' [9]:

> Yes, Google indexes dynamically generated web pages, including .asp pages, .php pages, and pages with question marks in their URLs. However, these pages can cause problems for our crawler and may be ignored. If you're concerned that your dynamically generated pages are being ignored, you may want to consider creating static copies of these pages for our crawler. If you do this, please be sure to include a robots.txt file that disallows the dynamic pages in order to ensure that these pages aren't seen as having duplicate content. In addition, you might consider creating and submitting a detailed Sitemap. This is an easy way for you to submit all your URLs to the Google index and get detailed reports about the visibility of your pages on Google. (It is better not to present duplicate information to the webcrawler because it may consider it to be an illegal trick to stir up PageRank.)

Google's advice may solve some of the problems, and a commercial site like Amazon will make sure that a search for any book title will also lead to the information stored in its database. But it is an illusion that search engines will ever be able to retrieve information from databases protected by passwords. This part of the 'deep web' will always be invisible for someone who cannot, or does not want to, pay for the information stored in it.

Notes

1. See: *http://www.dmoz.org/erz/editors/editor-types.html*
2. Based on Sikkenga, H., Waart, P. van and Hofstede, M. (2001) 'Als je niet weet waar je het zoeken moet: een onderzoek naar Nederlandstalige WebWebWijzers'. [If you do not know where to find it: a research into Dutch Webguides], *Informatie Professional*, 5, 6: 18–31 (in Dutch).
3. A good introduction can be found in Rogers, I. (2002) 'The Google pagerank algorithm and how it works', web article. Available from: *http://www.sirgroane.net/google-page-rank/*
4. See: *http://www.google.com/onceuponatime/technology/pigeon rank.html*
5. Invisible-web.net indexes 0.2 per cent, lii.org 3.1 per cent and completeplanet.com reaches 15.6 per cent.

References

[1] Baeza-Yates, R. and Ribeiro-Neto, B. (1999), *Modern Information Retrieval*. Harlow: Addison-Wesley, p. 382.
[2] Lewandowski, D. (2005), 'Web searching, search engines and information retrieval', in *Information Services & Use*, 25: 137–47.
[3] Page, L., Brin, S., Motwani, R. and Winograd, T. (1999), 'The PageRank citation ranking: bringing order to the web', web article. Available from: *http://dbpubs. stanford.edu:8090/pub/1999-66*

[4] Rogers, I. (2002), 'The Google Pagerank Algorithm and How It Works', web article. Available from: *http://www.sirgroane.net/google-page-rank/*

[5] Langville, A.N. and Meer, C.D. (2006), *Google's PageRank and Beyond: the Science of Search Engine Rankings*. Princeton: Princeton University Press.

[6] Cutts, M. (2005), 'How does Google collect and rank results?', web article. Available from: *http://www2.curriculum.edu.au/scis/connections/issue_58/how_does_google_collect_and_rank_results.html*

[7] Bin H., Patel, M., Zhen, Z. and Chen-Chuan Chang, K. (2007), 'Accessing the Deep Web', *Communications of the ACM*, 50, 5: 95–101.

[8] McCown, F., Liu, X., Nelson, M.L. and Zubair, M. (2006), 'Search engine coverage of the OAI-PMH corpus', *IEEE Internet Computing*, 10, 2: 66–73.

[9] *http://www.google.com/support/webmasters/bin/answer.py?answer=34431&topic=8522*

12

The Semantic Web

I have a dream for the web . . . and it has two parts.

(Tim Berners-Lee [1])

Abstract: In the vision of Tim Berners-Lee the web is moving towards the Semantic Web in the near future, and further on to the Web of Reasoning. The first stages of the web were the Web of Documents (Web 1.0) and the Social Web (Web 2.0). The main instruments to realize the Semantic Web have already been developed: XML, RDF, etc. The first Semantic Web browsers are already operational. The Simple Knowledge Organization System (SKOS) guarantees that the vast knowledge hidden in the traditional instruments libraries used for indexing, i.e. subject headings, thesauri and classifications, can contribute to the realization of the Semantic Web.

Key words: Semantic Web, SKOS, ontologies, folksonomies, XML, Resource Description Framework.

Introduction

By now, you have read in almost every chapter about the Semantic Web. Probably the only conclusion you have drawn from these passages is that it must be something promising – and it certainly is. The Semantic Web is the brainchild of Tim Berners-Lee, the father of the World Wide Web. He was not satisfied with the way the World Wide Web turned out to be and kept on chasing the dreams he had when he invented the web in 1989–90 at the CERN (Conseil Européen pour la Recherche Nucléaire). Since the mid 1990s he has been working at the World Wide Web Consortium, which still is the driving force behind the activities that should lead to the realization of the Semantic Web.

The patrons of the Semantic Web rewrite the history of the web in their own way – which is different from the chronology the Topic Maps people use:

- 1990: Tim Berners-Lee invents the World Wide Web with the first webpage.

- 1993: Marc Andreessen launches Mosaic, the first popular graphical browser, precursor of Netscape Navigator.

- 1994: founding of the World Wide Web Consortium (*http://www.w3.org*); Tim Berners-Lee launches the idea of the Semantic Web.

- 1998: the World Wide Web Consortium launches XML.

- 1999–present: the standards for the Semantic Web are being developed.

The Semantic Web is supposed to be closer to the initial concept of the web, which does not mean that it is a kind of regression to the situation at the beginning of the 1990s. In the eyes of the Semantic Web patrons the web took off in a more or less wrong direction. We will deal with their criticism in the next paragraph. The history of the web could also be divided into larger periods:

- Web 1.0: the actual web, consisting of mainly HTML pages.
- Web 2.0: the Social Web, the interactive web (blogs, wikis, photo and video sites, folksonomies, etc.)
- Web 3.0: the Semantic Web, the web of data.
- Web 4.0: the web of reasoning, the intelligent web.

Web 2.0 came after Web 1.0 and is flourishing now, but both exist next to one another. Web 3.0 has not been realized yet, but it is planned and prepared. We will discuss the timetable more closely later.

The criticism against the actual web

Although everybody recognizes that Web 1.0 is of enormous value and impact, some criticism can be formulated:

- The actual web consists mainly of an enormous amount of HTML pages. A lot of people have learnt to write and publish HTML pages in order to get their message published on the web.[1] Some have mastered HTML code, but many others just grab the nearest HTML editor and generate whatever pages they like. Most of them do not care if their web pages are not well formed, do not contain metatags, etc., as long as their message is understandable for their readers, i.e. humans who read web pages almost in the same way they read paper documents. Browsers add to this by being very tolerant towards HTML.

- HTML is a layout tool: HTML tags have little or no relation to the meaning of the text. The consequence is that it is extremely difficult to develop programs that can 'understand' HTML pages. If we want to process the information in web pages, there should be more structure.

- A searcher using a search engine mostly gets thousands of links to web pages as an answer to his question. He can open every page and read through it in the hope that it contains the information he wants. He will be trapped in each page: if he wants to get more information, he can only follow the links the author offers him. Although the ranking mechanism that search engines apply may be sophisticated, there is no way of selecting relevant information from different pages and getting it presented in a comprehensive way in one or in a few screens.

In his autobiographic book *Weaving the Web* [2] Tim Berners-Lee wrote: 'I have a dream for the web . . . and it has two parts. In the first part, the web becomes a much more powerful means for collaboration between people. I have always imagined the information space as something to which everyone has immediate and intuitive access, and not just to browse, but to create.'

Of course, since 1989 we have come a long way, but web applications still have serious limitations. Programs were developed to process information from web pages and online catalogues, but the actual web is not a reliable source for information processing. Tim Berners-Lee writes:

> The trick of getting a computer to extract information from an online catalogue is just that: a trick. It is known as *screen scraping* – trying to salvage something usable from information that is now in a form suitable only for humans. It is tenuous because the catalogue could change overnight – for example, putting the ISBN number where the price used to be – and the automatic broker would be confused [3].

We can see a lot of sympathy towards Web 2.0, the Social Web, in texts dealing with the relation between Web 2.0 and the Semantic Web. There seems to be hope that it will be possible to recover, i.e. process automatically the unique information which is stored massively in Web 2.0 applications. The difference between Web 1.0 and Web 2.0, seen from a technical point of view, is that is it more feasible to get structure into Web 2.0 applications than there can ever be in Web 1.0 applications. This may need some explanation because it probably sounds rather contradictory.

Folksonomies may look like chaos itself: everybody can put pictures, video films, bookmarks, diary fragments, etc. on the web. In many cases they can also tag it any way they want and label their photos with meaningless tags like 'me', 'at home', 'no comment', '005', 'IMGP873', etc. This goes on, day by day, on a massive scale. Flickr used to tell how many pictures had been uploaded in the last minute. This usually was a number in the range of 4000 or 5000 on a slow day and 7000 or more on a busy one, which will add up to more than 3 million in one month. Still, this is less chaotic than the HTML pages published in Web 1.0, because of the simple fact that sites like Flickr are very well structured. If such a site decides to add some tool that enables automatic processing of its content, millions of photos can be processed with applications that use that tool. This is not possible with Web 1.0 sites: you would have to ask each author to add this tool to his site.

When the Semantic Web is fully realized the web will have become a huge database with structured information; now it is still an unstructured pile of documents. Social sites and tagging at least bring some structure.

Planning Web 3.0

Suppose the web is indeed this large structured database. You could formulate complex queries and get an answer in one web page instead of going through 20 000 or more links to pages that might contain only a part of the answer. A typical question that could be answered by a Semantic Web engine would be: 'Which articles on telemarketing were written in 2007 by authors working in companies with less than 100 employees?'.[2] If you wanted to find the answer to this question using actual search engines and databases, you would have to take many actions and therefore it would be rather time consuming. The question can be translated into a few tasks you would have to fulfil:

1. Find all articles in bibliographic databases or on the web dealing with telemarketing written in 2007.

2. Make a list of the affiliations of the authors of those articles, if available, and check the names of the authors of whom no affiliation is mentioned, in bibliographic databases, in databases about companies, or on the web.

3. Check which of the firms you found this way have less than 100 employees, using economical databases, the websites of those firms, etc.

4. Make a list of all results.

The example Tim Berners-Lee uses in his book *Weaving the Web* is: 'Did any baseball team play yesterday in a place where the temperature was 22°C?' [2: 180]. Answering this would mean that you would have to make a list of all places where baseball teams played and one of all places where the temperature was 22°C; you would have to compare those lists (manually or by means of some computer program). Tim Berners-Lee notes: 'A simple search would have returned an endless list of possible answers that the human would have to wade through' [2: 180].

When the Semantic Web is fully operational, these questions could be answered in seconds and the result would be presented in a simple webpage. In a way this is comparable to what we know now as federated search: instead of searching all the databases that are available in a library, we launch a query to the federated search engine which executes the search in all databases and presents a list of answers from every one containing items that correspond with our search terms. But compared to what should be possible in Web 3.0 this is still very primitive because complex questions cannot be answered by federated search engines. Even the opposite is the case: federated search engines are forced to ignore all indexes that apply only to one database, e.g. thesauri: they are limited to using basic search indexes like words from title, words from abstract, author names, etc.

In order to transform the web into a giant structured database a lot of new instruments are needed. Some have already been realized, others are still to come. There is a well-known scheme with the building blocks for Web 3.0 from a presentation Tim Berners-Lee held in 2000 [4], illustrated in Figure 12.1. Some of these building blocks are already built, others still need a lot of work. We will give a brief (and non-technical) overview of main instruments. Technical details can be found at *www.w3.org*.

Figure 12.1 Building blocks for the Semantic Web

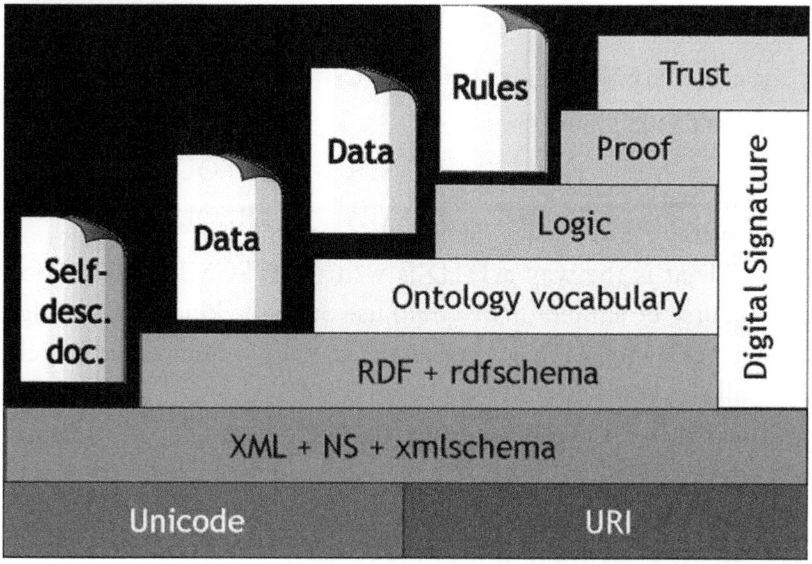

XML and XML schema

XML (eXtensible Markup Language) had been developed by the end of the 1990s. Although some people may still think XML is a more advanced HTML, it is not. HTML is just a set of tags to encode the layout of a webpage. Technically HTML is an application of SGML (the Standard Generalized Markup Language) whereas XML is a subset of SGML. This means that everybody can (in principle) make his own application in XML. You cannot make your own HTML; you can only use it to put some layout into your web pages. To define one's own tags is of course not easy and it was even harder in the beginning when you had to write a DTD (Document Type Definition), a kind of table in which every tag is defined, before you could start doing anything with your application. This is a very technical activity since it assumes good knowledge of another encoding system, the Extended Backus–Naur Form (EBNF). In order to say that you wanted a tag <publisher> with sub-tags for the city and the name, you would have to write something like:

<!ELEMENT publisher EMPTY>

<!ATTLIST publisher

    publisherPlace   CDATA   #REQUIRED

    publisherName   CDATA   #REQUIRED>

That is the way a DTD is written in SGML. It would of course be simpler if we could use only one kind of encoding. This is why the XML schema language was invented which allows you to define your own XML tags using XML itself. XML is the basic language for the Semantic Web because tags defined in XML relate to the content of the data and because it is machine readable. The whole communication on the Semantic Web will use XML.

Resource Description Framework

The Resource Description Framework (RDF) is a way to describe resources on the web. Following an example from the *RDF Primer* [5], a statement about a webpage, e.g.

http://www.example.org/index.html was written by John Smith

can be read as:

http://www.example.org/index.html has a creator whose value is John Smith

and can be analysed as:

- the *subject* is the URL 'http://www.example.org/index. html'
- the *predicate* is the word 'creator'
- the *object* is the phrase 'John Smith'

and because the vocabulary that defines 'creator' and the information about this 'John Smith' is also on the web, we can translate this into:

- subject http://www.example.org/index.html
- predicate http://purl.org/dc/elements/1.1/creator
- object http://www.example.org/staffid/85740

All we need now is a way to translate this into XML, the basic language of Web 3.0. This is done by means of the RDF schema. A Web 3.0 search engine, which of course should be able to read XML, will 'know' what is said about documents because it can interpret RDF – and because (this is an essential assumption) every document is on the web.

For Tim Berners-Lee, RDF is vital for the Semantic Web. In *Weaving the Web* he writes: 'If HTML and the web made all the online documents look like one huge book, RDF, schema, and inference languages will make all the data in the world look like one huge database' [6]. Time and again he defends RDF against the possible criticism that it might be too powerful:

> When we unleash the power of RDF so that it allows us to express inference rules, we can still constrain it so that it is not such an expressive language that it will frighten people. The inference rules won't have to be a full programming language. They will be analyzable and separable, and should not present a threat. However, for automating some real-life tasks, the language will have to become more powerful [7].

Ontologies

Ontologies play a vital rule in the Semantic Web because they provide a web of meaning. If we link one ontology to many others we get an enormous web consisting of structured relations between all kinds of subjects and objects, persons, etc. linked to these subjects. The key to getting meaning into the web lies in the network of well-developed ontologies.

Web 3.0 query language

It is not enough to have ontologies and encoded information: we also need tools to search the Semantic Web, i.e. search engines that can take their advantage of ontologies and that can read and compare XML coded information. The actual search engines cannot. In order to retrieve and compare information from different web sources, we should use a language that is comparable to what SQL is for relational databases. The Word Wide Web Consortium has already developed these query languages:

- SPARQL: a query language for RDF documents (*http://www.w3.org/TR/rdf-sparql-query*)

- XQuery: a query language of XML documents (*http://www.w3.org/TR/xquery*)

Until now, it has only been possible to see the effect of these languages at some experimental sites:

The friend-of-a-friend project

The friend-of-a-friend project[3] is an example of a social network. The search engine retrieves all friends of a person, with their home pages, e-mail addresses and other relevant information. It also retrieves all organizations the person is engaged in, all websites he contributes to, etc. In principle, these data do not come out of a database, but are harvested all over the web.

The Disco-Hyperdata browser

This experimental browser,[4] developed at the Freie Universität Berlin, finds all relevant information about a person or a subject on the web and presents it in a comprehensive page, as in Figure 12.2.

Semantic search engines

Semantic search engines try to bring relevant information together in a comprehensive way. Instead of giving a list of web pages based on the fact that our search term occurs at least one time in them, they make a selection of the most relevant pages. How they do it is explained at *http://hakia.com*, a search engine which claims to be leading in Semantic

Figure 12.2 Example of search results in the Disco-Hyperdata browser

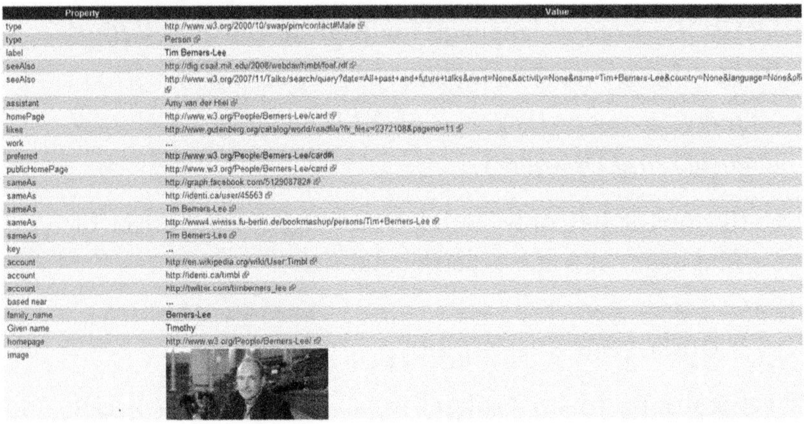

Property	Value
type	http://www.w3.org/2000/10/swap/pim/contact#Male
type	Person
label	Tim Berners-Lee
seeAlso	http://dig.csail.mit.edu/2008/webdav/timbl/foaf.rdf
seeAlso	http://www.w3.org/2007/11/Talks/search/query?date=All+past+and+future+talks&event=None&activity=None&name=Tim+Berners-Lee&country=None&language=None&offi
assistant	Amy van der Hiel
homePage	http://www.w3.org/People/Berners-Lee/card
likes	http://www.gutenberg.org/catalog/world/readfile?fk_files=2372108&pageno=11
work	...
preferred	http://www.w3.org/People/Berners-Lee/card#i
publicHomePage	http://www.w3.org/People/Berners-Lee/card
sameAs	http://graph.facebook.com/512908782#
sameAs	http://identi.ca/user/45563
sameAs	Tim Berners-Lee
sameAs	http://www4.wiwiss.fu-berlin.de/bookmashup/persons/Tim+Berners-Lee
sameAs	Tim Berners-Lee
key	...
account	http://en.wikipedia.org/wiki/User:Timbl
account	http://identi.ca/timbl
account	http://twitter.com/timberners_lee
based near	...
family_name	Berners-Lee
Given name	Timothy
homepage	http://www.w3.org/People/Berners-Lee/
image	

Web technology. Hakia sums up ten characteristics which make it different from 'normal' search engines like Google:

1. It can handle morphological variations: it should not matter whether you enter a search term in singular, plural, etc. Words like 'rain', or 'raining' or 'rained' should all lead to the same result.
2. It can handle synonyms. 'Disease' should be understood as a synonym of 'illness', etc.
3. It can handle generalizations: a question like 'Which disease has the symptom of coughing?' must retrieve all diseases where coughing is at least one of the symptoms.
4. It matches concepts; it can build a relation between e.g. 'headache' and 'migraine'.
5. It matches knowledge. Here Hakia explains: 'Very similar to the previous item, a semantic search engine is expected to have embedded knowledge and use it to bring relevant results (swine flu = H1N1, flu = influenza.)'
6. It can handle natural language queries and questions.

7. It points to the most relevant paragraphs or sections in a document: it does not stop when a document with certain keywords is retrieved; it selects the most relevant parts of it.

8. The user can enter queries in a natural way; he or she does not need to use Boolean operators or quotation marks.

9. It does not rely on user behaviour, statistics, linking etc. It analyses the content of documents.

10. It analyses its own performances. It does not rely on the popularity of a page, but on how well it matches the question.

All this is very ambitious, but is it also working? Does it give e.g. more satisfactory answers than Google? Let's try some simple questions and hope that we will find a satisfactory answer in the top ranked sites, i.e. on the first page (because this is usually what people do):

Question	Hakia	Google
Where can I rent a bike in Brussels?	Satisfactory	Satisfactory
What is a cure against coughing?	No answer	Satisfactory, but only pages with 'coughing'
How far is it to Amsterdam?	Site with travelling guides of Amsterdam	Sites with distance calculators in which Amsterdam appears (containing the words 'how', 'far' and 'Amsterdam')
What kind of leather is suitable for shoes?	Not satisfactory	Satisfactory
How many days did it rain in Holland in 2010?	Not satisfactory	Not satisfactory
Why is my laptop running hot?	Satisfactory	Satisfactory

This is not a scientific test. We can expect that standard tests with standard questions will be developed. These naïve questions at least show that the non-semantic search engine Google is not doing badly. We would expect Hakia to know that 'the Netherlands' is a synonym for 'Holland' and we would also expect that it knows some cure for coughing since most of its own examples are medical. Obviously more work needs to be done in order to get better results for these kind of questions in natural language. This does not mean that Hakia is not a good search engine. On the contrary: I rely on it when I want answers with high precision. Usually those searches are not the kind of questions I asked here, but one or more keywords. Hakia normally gives me only sites with high precision and, indeed, highlights the relevant paragraphs or phrases in it. Undoubtedly improvement can be expected, but there is still time for it – according to the timetable for the Semantic Web.

A timetable for the Semantic Web

In an interesting PowerPoint presentation Nova Spivak gives an outline of the past and the future of the web [8]:

Period	Web	Indexing and retrieval
1990–2000	Web 1.0, the WWW	keyword search
2000–10	Web 2.0, the Social Web	tagging
2010–20	Web 3.0, the Semantic Web	semantic search
2020–30	Web 4.0, the Intelligent Web	reasoning

At this moment we are living the hype of the Social Web, where everybody can put information on the web and add (meaningful or meaningless) tags to it. These techniques are being integrated into all kinds of web-based applications, e.g. library catalogues or museum sites. Meanwhile the instruments for the Semantic Web are developed, but it will be a long way until the Semantic Web is fully operational. Some problems need to be solved first:

- More standards must be developed.

- These standards must be translated into computer programs.

- A lot of information has to be encoded in view of the standards.

But even if all this is realized, there are still some fundamental issues to deal with:

Privacy issues

Many examples of what the Semantic Web could be take it for granted that the necessary information is freely available on the web. This is not the case: a lot of information is stored in corporate databases which will never be opened for the public. In real life, a friend-of-a-friend project will constantly collide with 'access denied' messages.

The chaotic nature of the web

To realize the Semantic Web we need to have highly structured documents. They should correspond to the XML, RDF and other standards. It is questionable if the majority of the documents on the web will ever be structured in this way. Since the beginning of the 1990s people have uploaded documents on the web that are not structured in a way a semantic search engine can make sense of them: word processor files, PowerPoint presentations, badly designed HTML pages, etc. These documents not only stay on the web, but the same kind of unstructured information is added every day in a massive way.

The discrepancy between ontologies and Web 2.0 tagging

Web 2.0 is successful because it is fun: you can tag whatever you want in whatever way you like. Some techniques may be used to get a grip on this chaos, e.g. comparing similarities, differences and synchronicity between tags. Even if we can develop instruments to 'normalise' them, they are still very different from ontologies which are built according to a set of rigid rules.

Ontologies' weak spot

But there is more: ontologies are fundamental for Web 3.0 because they form a web of meaning. Navigating through ontologies and from one ontology to another would allow us to refine our search until we reach our goal. The formal rules of how to build an ontology may be well defined in a standard and integrated into ontology editors, but neither one or the other can prevent me from making a completely nonsensical ontology. Let's not be naïve: many people are doing their best to contribute in a positive and meaningful way to the world, but a lot of idiots, criminals and socially frustrated people find satisfaction in sabotaging those efforts.

The Semantic Web and traditional library instruments

The Semantic Web will rely on 'linked data'. In order to link data, computer programs must be able to deal with the kind of problems thesauri builders know all too well: synonyms, homonyms, relations between terms etc. At the turn of the century things very much looked like all cards were put on ontologies, hence the complaints by librarians that their expertise was ignored and that the wheel was reinvented all over again, as Dagobert Soergel and others wrote (see Chapter 7).

Now the knowledge that is stored in thesauri, subject headings and classifications is fully recognized by the World Wide Web Consortium as important building blocks for the Semantic Web. The only practical obstacle to extracting that knowledge from thesauri, subject headings and classifications is their format. Although by now most of them are on the web, they all come in a different way. Some are just PDF files, others are stored in a database, still others are just codes in HTML etc. Semantic Web applications need information they can read, i.e. information coded in XML and, if possible, RDF.

The Simple Knowledge Organization System (SKOS) is meant to be the missing link between Semantic Web applications and the traditional library indexing tools. As the World Wide Web Consortium puts it on their website:

> Today W3C announces a new standard that builds a bridge between the world of knowledge organization systems – including thesauri, classifications, subject headings, taxonomies, and folksonomies – and the linked data community, bringing benefits to both. Libraries, museums, newspapers, government portals,

237

enterprises, social networking applications, and other communities that manage large collections of books, historical artifacts, news reports, business glossaries, blog entries, and other items can now use Simple Knowledge Organization System (SKOS) to leverage the power of linked data [9].

As you can see here thesauri, etc., are put on the same level as folksonomies: all together fall into the category of the kind of indexing systems that are not structured according to the new rules, as opposed to ontologies which were coded in XML and RDF from the beginning. Now SKOS should make them accessible. The final SKOS 'recommendation', i.e. standard in the terminology of the World Wide Web Consortium, was published in 2009, which is relatively late in the development of the instruments leading toward the Semantic Web, hence the fear of some during the previous years that traditional indexing tools would be left out.

In future, more and more thesauri, subject heading systems and classifications will have a SKOS counterpart next to the readable form, as now already is the case in e.g. the Australian Schools Online Thesaurus. The descriptor 'history' is displayed in HTML as in Figure 12.3. The SKOS version looks like this:

```
<?xml version='1.0' encoding='UTF-8'?>
<rdf:RDF
xmlns:owl='http://www.w3.org/2002/07/owl#'
xmlns:cycAnnot='http://sw.cyc.com/CycAnnotations_v1#'
xmlns:cyc='http://sw.cyc.com/concept/'
xmlns:dbpedia='http://dbpedia.org/resource/'
```

```
xmlns:ctag='http://commontag.org/ns#'
xmlns:opencyc=http://sw.opencyc.org/concept/'
xmlns:foaf='http://xmlns.com/foaf/0.1/'
xmlns:csw='http://semantic-web.at/ontologies/csw.owl#'
xmlns:rdfs='http://www.w3.org/2000/01/rdf-schema#'
xmlns:rdf='http://www.w3.org/1999/02/22-rdf-syntax-ns#'
xmlns:skos='http://www.w3.org/2004/02/skos/corey#'
xmlns:xsd='http://www.w3.org/2001/XMLSchema#'
xmlns:dc='http://purl.org/dc/elements/1.1/'
xmlns:freebase='http://rdf.freebase.com/ns/'
xmlns:dcterms='http://purl.org/dc/terms/'
xmlns:tags='http://www.holygoat.co.uk/owl/redwood/
    0.1/tags/'>

<rdf:Description rdf:about='http://vocabulary.curriculum.
    edu.au/scot/317'>
<rdf:type rdf:resource='http://www.w3.org/2004/02/skos/
    core#Concept'/>
<skos:inScheme rdf:resource='http://vocabulary.curriculum.
    edu.au/scot'/>
<skos:topConceptOf>http://vocabulary.curriculum.edu.au/
    scot</skos:topConceptOf>
<skos:prefLabel xml:lang='en'>History</skos:prefLabel>
<skos:altLabel xml:lang='en'>Humanities (History)
    </skos:altLabel>
<dcterms:issued rdf:datatype='http://www.w3.org/2001/
    XMLSchema#dateTime'>2005-02-01T00:00:00</dcterms:
    issued>
```

```
<skos:narrower rdf:resource='http://vocabulary.curriculum.
    edu.au/scot/11627'/>

<skos:narrower rdf:resource='http://vocabulary.curriculum.
    edu.au/scot/12482'/>

<skos:narrower rdf:resource='http://vocabulary.curriculum.
    edu.au/scot/3989'/>

<skos:narrower rdf:resource='http://vocabulary.curriculum.
    edu.au/scot/4676'/>

<skos:related rdf:resource='http://vocabulary.curriculum.
    edu.au/scot/6837'/>

<skos:narrower rdf:resource='http://vocabulary.curriculum.
    edu.au/scot/15002'/>

<skos:altLabel xml:lang='en'>The past</skos:altLabel>

<skos:altLabel xml:lang='en'>Past events</skos:altLabel>

<dcterms:contributor>Education Services Australia Ltd
    </dcterms:contributor>

<skos:narrowerTransitive rdf:resource='http://vocabulary.
    curriculum.edu.au/scot/1382'/>

<skos:narrowerTransitive rdf:resource='http://vocabulary.
    curriculum.edu.au/scot/7829'/>

<skos:narrowerTransitive rdf:resource='http://vocabulary.
    curriculum.edu.au/scot/15041'/>

<skos:narrowerTransitive rdf:resource='http://vocabulary.
    curriculum.edu.au/scot/15040'/>

<skos:narrowerTransitive rdf:resource='http://vocabulary.
    curriculum.edu.au/scot/15042'/>

<skos:narrowerTransitive rdf:resource='http://vocabulary.
    curriculum.edu.au/scot/15043'/>
```

```
<skos:narrowerTransitive rdf:resource='http://vocabulary.
  curriculum.edu.au/scot/11536'/>
<skos:narrowerTransitive rdf:resource='http://vocabulary.
  curriculum.edu.au/scot/1156'/>
<skos:narrowerTransitive rdf:resource='http://vocabulary.
  curriculum.edu.au/scot/11626'/>
<skos:narrowerTransitive rdf:resource='http://vocabulary.
  curriculum.edu.au/scot/11694'/>
<skos:narrowerTransitive rdf:resource='http://vocabulary.
  curriculum.edu.au/scot/12035'/>
<skos:narrowerTransitive rdf:resource='http://vocabulary.
  curriculum.edu.au/scot/5805'/>
<skos:narrowerTransitive rdf:resource='http://vocabulary.
  curriculum.edu.au/scot/15044'/>
<skos:prefLabel xml:lang='zh'>历史</skos:prefLabel>
<skos:prefLabel xml:lang='ko'>역사</skos:prefLabel>
<skos:prefLabel xml:lang='ar'>خيرات</skos:prefLabel>
<skos:prefLabel xml:lang='de'>Geschichte</skos:prefLabel>
<skos:prefLabel xml:lang='fr'>Histoire</skos:prefLabel>
<skos:prefLabel xml:lang='es'>Historia</skos:prefLabel>
<skos:prefLabel xml:lang='ja'>歴史</skos:prefLabel>
</rdf:Description>

</rdf:RDF>
```

Starting from here Semantic Web programs can follow the links to the narrower and related terms. Learning how to build a thesaurus wasn't such a bad idea after all . . .

| Figure 12.3 | The Australian Schools Online Thesaurus (*http:// scot.curriculum.edu.au/*) |

Notes

1. It was not Tim Berners-Lee's intention that someone would have to take the trouble of learning HTML in order to compose a document; he wanted browsers that at the same time were HTML editors.
2. 'The "semantic web" will make finding answers online as simple as asking the right question' is the title of an article on Web 3.0 by Jim Giles in *New Scientist* (vol. 198, issue 2658, 31 May 2008, pp. 26–7).
3. An example can be seen at: *http://xml.mfd-consult.dk/foaf/ explorer/?foaf=http://danbri.org/foaf.rdf*
4. See: *http://www4.wiwiss.fu-berlin.de/bizer/ng4j/disco/*

References

[1] Berners-Lee, T. (2000), *Weaving the Web: the Original Design and Ultimate Destiny of the World Wide Web.* New York: HarperBusiness, p. 157.

[2] Ibid.

[3] Ibid.

[4] *http://www.w3.org/2000/Talks/1206-xml2k-tbl/ slide10-0.html*

[5] *http://www.w3.org/TR/REC-rdf-syntax/*

[6] Berners-Lee, T. (2000), *Weaving the Web: the Original Design and Ultimate Destiny of the World Wide Web.* New York: HarperBusiness, p. 186.

[7] Ibid. pp. 190–1.

[8] http://*novaspivack.typepad.com/nova_spivacks_weblog/ files/nova_spivack_semantic_web_talk.ppt*

[9] *http://www.w3.org/2004/02/skos/*

Index

Printed and bound by CPI Group (UK) Ltd, Croydon, CR0 4YY

03/10/2024

01040437-0011